In Love
With *Marriage*

Discovering the Reasons Why We Married

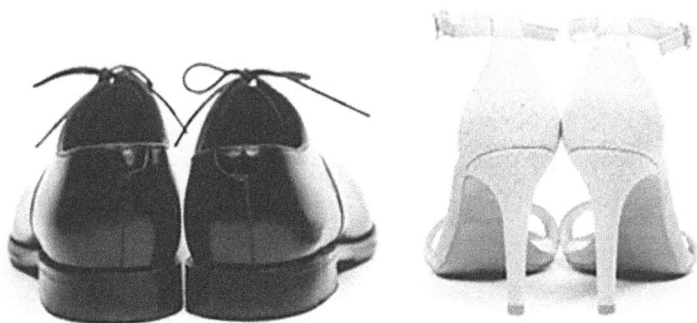

JESSIE GARCIA

In Love
with Marriage

The story of one man's journey to understand why he married by going through his life events.

Jessie Garcia

PTP
Pure Thoughts Publishing LLC

www.PureThoughtsPublishing.com

.

Table of Contents

Dedication

In Love with Marriage is first and foremost giving glory to God by which has been the foundation of my strength and reason for writing this book.

I dedicate this to Yomaira, my wife, whom through our difficulties has been a voice of reason. Through her strengths and weaknesses she encouraged me to find myself.

It is through her that I have chosen to discover myself.

This is also dedicated to my son, Sebastian, whom I love dearly. He has been a wonderful blessing and gift from God.

In special recognition to my mother and grandmother for never giving up on me.

To my Pastor Dr. R. Villalpando and the Kingdom Embassy for their continual love and support.

Introduction

Have you ever been in a position that you have had to ask yourself: "Why did I get married?" Have you ever questioned whether or not you made the right decision in choosing to marry your spouse? Does the question; "Why didn't I wait, or why didn't I marry so and so; or worse: Why did I not listen to my parents," keep you up at night?

If you are reading this and are faith-based, it is easy to question yourself: "Was my spouse sent from God, or was it not His will for me to have had married them?" There's nothing wrong with questioning yourself. It's the start of a process to help you discover yourself and make the necessary changes to save your marriage or your sanity.

There are plenty of challenges that come with marriage, whether you have been married for more than five years or less. Marriage is a lifelong commitment of discovering each other as the years bring changes and challenges. It was not designed to be a one player game; it's a team, and together you can overcome the challenges. Marriage can be great, but it is a lot of continuous work!

The dating process is designed for you to discover your partner before marriage, with the intention of building a trust to constructively discuss your differences before marriage. This will also aide after marriage .

when the communication between couples shows sign that it is breaking down. Often, one spouse will either say "we never talk anymore" or "you don't understand me".

The problem with marriage is not that it is an institution, meaning, that as a married couple, you have to conduct yourselves according to the morals and values of marriage. The problem often stems from either not knowing what marriage is or marrying for the wrong reasons.

Some were never taught or failed to discover what it meant to enter into a committed relationship or the covenant of marriage.

During difficult times in a relationship, it is ok to question certain areas in your life that you feel are not working. When everything is working great in the marriage, it is easy for you to find all the right reasons as to why you chose to marry your spouse. During times of difficulties, you can find even more reasons to justify why you would want to separate from the marriage? The words: "Till death do us part," are often forgotten when the marriage faces challenges.

Before you make the decision to separate, or if you're already separated, I want you to ask yourself, "Why did you get married?" I want you to think about the question for a minute. "Why did you get married?" The most common response is: "Because I was in love with the person." Another common response is: "I married my best friend." Some just say, "Because it felt like the right thing to do."

If love was the reason why couples get married, why is love the first to leave the marriage?

When couples begin to have issues within their marriage, it is so easy to see the faults in their spouse but fail to understand or accept that they also played a major role as to why things were not working. You cannot fix a problem until you understand where the problem is coming from. You cannot get to the root of a problem until you dig. Digging involves time, hard work and drilling through messy emotions, but once you get to the root, you can identify the injury to the relationship. Then you are able to fix and repair the issues.

We all have our own idea(s) of how we would like (or want) the marriage to be. They may be different from that of your spouse, but together, you can come to terms with what the "ideal marriage" you want to have together. The concept of marriage, meaning, taking your idea of marriage and making it a reality is not always how we plan it. Plans always change…consciously or unconsciously.

My journey has been filled with obstacles and struggles. I had to dig deep within my soul to discover myself and identify why my life was met with so much difficulty.

I have come to terms and accepted my mistakes and failures. My marriage struggled not because of the mistakes that my ex-wife and I committed, but because I discovered that I was more in love with the idea of marriage and did not understand the concept.

I want to share with you my journey as I had to dig deep into my roots to discover what was hidden down the dirty hole. I invite you to share my struggles and pain, with the intent to show you how they affected my marriage! Once I discovered how damaged my roots were, I could identify how they influenced the decisions that I made and how they affected my marriage!

There was much pain involved in digging, but once I was able to overcome the pain of my past, I was able to be free from all resentment, guilt, shame, and anger that I had buried for many years. It was then that I was able to find forgiveness and also able to understand what it meant to truly forgive someone who has hurt you and to be freed from that burden.

My first marriage ended in divorce. I did not think my past failures would enter into my next marriage causing conflicts, but they subtly found their way in. At the point of repeating history, my wife asked me: "Why did you marry me?" I loved her very much, so it was easy for me to respond without hesitation; "Because I loved you!" I thought it would have made her happy, and in my mind, I pictured her giving me a hug, and telling me that she loved me as well. Instead, she asked me, "If you love me, why are we continually hurting each other?" I could not respond.

She asked me to give her a better answer. "What better answer was there, isn't love is supposed to be the reason we're married?" I did not understand. I did not know what answer she was looking for. She then asked me to spend some time by myself to think of the question. She probably knew something that I didn't know, but refused to talk more about the matter.

It is important that you find the strength within you to discover yourself as I did to save yourself and your marriage. This can only be accomplished through enduring the hardships and pain involved in digging up your past. But, once you can overcome the past, you will be a stronger person that is able to love freely.

Chapter 1

In the Beginning

Growing up in the late '80s and early '90s was great! But…I can honestly state that it caused some damage to my psyche. Coming from a family headed by a single parent with seven children, life did not always turn out as I wanted. As a child, I was introduced to television shows like: The Cosby Show with the Huxtable's, Full House, Family Matters, and Step by Step. I would not know how much these sitcoms would influence me until years later.

Sitcoms for me were more than watching a thirty-minute happy ending, it was more about the desire of being part of a loving family. I wanted a family that would always come together to eat at the dinner table. A family that would be there for you when life presented itself with a terrible situation, or just the feeling of having someone to come home to even if you knew that coming home meant that you would be in trouble.

The idea of having a loving and supportive family should be everyone's desire regardless of what generation you come from, your race, or religion of preference. No one thinks about getting married only to end up divorced. Every couple wants to have a successful marriage. Everyone's idea of marriage can vary, but everyone wants to follow the same patterns: loving parents, a nice home, and a sense of belonging.

As a kid, I dreamed of having a mom that would take me to soccer or karate practice. A dad that loves his wife (my mom) and would be this funny guy that loved me, no matter what trouble I got myself into. I wanted to have a family just like those on the sitcoms.

The thing that impacted me the most was the idea of having my bedroom. In almost every sitcom, every child had their room regardless of how big the family was. Coming from a large family, I could only dream of having my own room and privacy. Having six siblings would never allow me the luxury of having my own room!

At one point in my life, my mother was renting a three-bedroom two-bathroom duplex. The three bedrooms seemed to work. The four boys were in one bedroom and the three girls were in the other bedroom, while mom often slept alone in her room or sometimes with my youngest sister. For a short time, everything worked out well. We managed to adjust to the situation.

Then, one year, one of my aunts was going through a divorce and came to live with us. She brought her six children with her (five girls and one boy). My aunt and her girls moved into my sisters' bedroom and my sisters slept in my mother's room. My male cousin slept in the room with all the boys.

Shortly after the new family arrangements, another aunt was going through a difficult situation and she moved in with her three daughters. The second aunt moved into the boys' bedroom and the boys slept in the living room. Nineteen people were living in a three-bedroom two-bathroom duplex. The square footage of the duplex was around nine hundred square feet. Looking back, I do not know how we survived! I complained when it was the eight of us but this was beyond belief.

When my aunts moved in, we had to find a way to manage. Everyone could feel the frustration of living in a small home with so many people. The five boys slept in the living room while all the girls were in the bedrooms. This situation lingered for a period of six months to a year. There is no way to describe how the bathroom situation worked.

Everyone had a small white trash bag with their clothes. The chests of drawers were split for everyone's underclothes and socks. Our situation was a bit different, my older brother, my younger brother, and I interchanged clothes. We did not have a trash bag of our own. My mom had a big black trash bag with all the boys' clothes that we shared.

I often hear people with no sibling's state: "I wish I had a big family, it would have been so much fun!" I think back to this time and say to myself: "No way would I ever want to have a big family". Big families come with so much drama and complications. I made a promise to myself that if I had the chance to have my own family, it would be small!

During middle school, I only had two pairs of pants and two shirts that I would interchange every other day: two khaki-colored pants and two shirts, one black and a white shirt. The white shirt had this odd-looking smiley face. I can look back and laugh that even back in the late 80's, emoji shirts were popular.

My mother would wash one set of clothes while we wore the other to school. I never noticed how monotonous it was until a classmate pointed out to me that I was wearing the same shirt all the time. I knew we were poor, but it did not register in my mind to the extent of how poor we were. I simply replied: "It's my favorite shirt."

At the beginning of my sixth grade, my brother and I started fighting over t-shirts. He was in the eighth grade and was more conscientious of his appearance. I remember in one of our fights that we ended up ripping a good shirt. It almost seemed pathetic that we would be fighting for clothing, but middle school kids can be cruel. We didn't have much clothes so, fighting over them was normal. I would often hide my shirts to keep them away from my brothers.

Shoes would have to last us all the school year and we never had backpacks. I never knew -until years later - when my mom would tell stories to my aunts or her friends that she would go to the Goodwill or Thrift stores to buy clothes for us. She would wash them or throw them into one of our trash bags because she knew that if we found out where she bought them from, we would not wear them. In middle school, if the kids knew your clothes came from the Goodwill, it was the end of your social life.

My mom would tell us stories about the extremes she had gone through with my sisters. In particular, one sister, who had curly hair, found that the brand name Pantene Pro V Shampoo and conditioner allowed her hair to be more manageable. The off brands usually left her hair dry and puffy. My mother could not afford that brand name shampoo, so, she would go to the dollar store and buy a similar off-brand, open the Pantene bottle and fill it with the off-brand just to fool my sister.

My sister would often throw fits of rage if she did not get her shampoo. To her, it was a matter of life or death. We never knew the extremes my mother went through to provide for us.

I could never understand how television shows like Rosanne often portrayed the family as being a low-income family yet having many luxuries. The family had what seemed a large home with a living room, a full-size kitchen, each child having their bedrooms, and a garage where Dan would be working on a car. Their low-income family was a middle-class family compared to our low-income family.

The duplex were we lived had an "open concept" floor plan. The living room was only able to fit a couch, loveseat, and a coffee table. The kitchen was a few feet away from the living room. The dining room was able to only fit a small table which seated four, but because the kitchen was small, it only allowed for three chairs because the fourth side of the table had to be pushed against the wall.

The fourth chair would be stored in one of the bedrooms and would be brought out to eat. Someone would always have to share a small piece of a corner to fit in the fourth person eating at the table. Dinner time was challenging! Because the kitchen was so small, we never ate as a family sitting around the table talking. There was never a grace given and we didn't talk about how our day went.

If there was talking, it was my mom rushing everyone to finish eating so that she could wash dishes and get everyone to bed. Fights were normal as one child was hungry and was rushing the other to finish so they could take a seat at the table. On other occasions, the three girls would eat at the table while the boys would eat in the living room.

We had no concept of "family-style" eating. My mother was never exposed to it as a child. It was just something that was done in the sitcoms. On Thanksgiving, we followed the same routine of taking turns eating at the table. My mother would usually cook and everyone would wait their turn to eat. We were never exposed to large family Thanksgiving dinners. Every now and then, our families would get together for the holidays, but someone would get offended and the party would end. It would take months, even years to get them talking again.

My mother was a very strong and hard-working woman. For several years, my mother worked a double shift just to try and make ends meet. She worked from 6:30 am until 11:30 pm. It was difficult for her with the kids, so she asked my older brother to help care for my siblings while at work. His response to her was that it was not his responsibility to be taking care of her kids. Hearing those words, I knew the responsibility would fall on me. I was eleven years old when I started helping my mom.

As my mother would leave for work, I would have to wake up early to help get my younger siblings ready for school and feed them. I walked the younger siblings to the elementary school and then walk to my school which was nearby. After school, I would pick them up and walk them home.

My mother worked long hours! She worked hard to make sure the bills were paid, and struggled to give us the best Christmas she could. She was always saving throughout the year with Christmas in mind. One year, she was able to buy us the Super Nintendo with the Mortal Combat game that we loved to play so much at the arcade.

I could only imagine the look on her face, knowing that it was worth all her sacrifices, just seeing us enjoy the game on Christmas. We were young and did not understand the hard work and sacrifices she made to put food on the table and keep a roof over our heads, but she did the best she could to provide us with a good life.

Over the years, I started to become angry with my mother. At the age of eleven, I started to take care of my siblings: got them to school, got them home safely, helped them with their homework, played outside with them, and fed them at mealtime. Mom would often leave instructions on how to cook the meal before she left for work. Some days, she would wake up early to cook and all we needed was to warm it in the microwave. I made sure they bathed, and went to bed. It was overwhelming!

In the early '90s, teenagers were able to go to the courthouse and apply for a work permit. This permit allowed underage kids to work during school hours. I was presented with an opportunity to work full time and it seemed to be a great opportunity not to pass up.

A friend from middle school was getting into some trouble just as I was. His mother worked in a manufacturing facility that assembled powerboat electrical wire harnesses. My friend's mother felt that school was not for us so she spoke to the owner of the company to give us an opportunity to work. The owner was open to hiring us at the age of fourteen on a trial basis. We worked for that company for over a year.

I battled my mother with my decision to work. She was against it, but I finally convinced her. I would often tell people that I was tired of seeing my mother working hard and long hours, and I wanted to help her. But... the truth was that I was tired of having the responsibility of taking care of my siblings. I was looking for a way out.

We were required to work a full forty-hour week at the rate of $4.25 an hour with the expectation of working overtime. It was my decision to quit school and go to work to help my mother! I would give her my entire paycheck with the exception of $15 for lunch during the week, and $10 I would give my friends mother for gas.

Before I quit school, I was getting into a lot of trouble! The school would call my mother on a daily basis because of a fight or because I would refuse to go to class. I was not a problematic young man; I was acting out because of all the difficulties I was dealing with at home. This was my way of dealing with the frustrations.

I was facing so many opposing forces to be successful in life. It made more sense for me to stop going to school and focus on helping the family more. At the time, I figured it was more beneficial for me to work than continue getting into trouble.

I never knew my father. My mother had two men in her life – for a short time – but none that I was proud to call my stepfather. One was for a couple of years the other drifted in and out of our lives for several years. She had other short term relationships before she eventually married my step-father, but all her relationships were either abusive or unstable.

Some of the relationships she was involved with either abused her or were abusive to my siblings and me. Some of her partners were either alcoholic or lazy. None of these men provided us with the stability of family life. They were not men who could teach my brothers and me to be a man or shape our characters in a beneficial way.

I had three uncles that would help my mom with my brothers and me every now and then. Our main influence came from the uncle that lived with my grandmother whom my mother allowed us to spend time with. He was a great man but had his battle with addictions. He was a mechanic. I enjoyed spending time with him working on cars. I felt proud of getting my hands covered in grease and running to show my mom that I helped fix a car. Spending time with my uncle was nice, until mid-day when the effects of the alcohol would take over and he became loud and aggressive.

Growing up without a father was difficult. It was difficult for me, so I cannot imagine how my brothers felt about the subject. It has been a taboo subject to speak about so we never brought up the discussion even to this day. There were many nights that I would stay awake imagining…how my life would be, if I had my father present in my life.

I would fantasize of having a father like Dan on the Rosanne show. Would he come home from work, get a beer and fix something? Would we spend time together working on a classic car in the garage waiting for me to turn sixteen and get my driver's license so we can enjoy the car together? Would he take the time to discipline me and guide me? Would he have taught me how to be a man? What was most important to me was: would he have taken the time to show me how to interact with girls?

This was an important part of life that I missed out on. I desired so much to have that father-son relationship! I admired my friend for having a father. His father would drink a six-pack of beer a day, but he was not a heavy alcoholic like my uncles. He had a job that he maintained for years and was responsible towards his family. They did not have a great relationship together but he was always present in his life. He was never abusive to his family even when he was drinking.

My mother had seven kids. She had four boys and three girls. The four boys came first, and the three girls followed. I wish I could say that we had a close relationship with each other, but the truth is… that we were not. It seemed as if everyone was always doing their own thing!

When I was in elementary school, my mother would always send me with my older brother. If he wanted to go out with his friends, she would allow him only on the condition that he took me with him. This would infuriate him!

He wanted to go out and have fun with his friends, not babysit. I do not know if this was her way of keeping him out of trouble or just her way of getting a break from seven kids. For a short time, we were inseparable, where he went, I went. His friends became my friends. I enjoyed being with my brother. He was daring and loved to fight.

We got into a lot of trouble together. For a couple of years, we became very close. I looked up to my brother. He was the only male role model I had that was always present. My brother was very athletic and into sports. He played football and baseball and he was good at it. I believed that my brother would have gone far with football – he had the right influence in his life. High school football was as far as he was able to play.

My mother was not financially able to help him further his career in football. The enrollment fee and all the equipment were expensive. The years that he played always ended with his team going into the district championship. He was a very handsome young man and had an athletic physic; many of the girls in school were attracted to him.

I was just the total opposite! I was short, skinny, with a goofy haircut and I lacked self-esteem. I wanted to be like him in every aspect of his life, but physically and mentally, there was no comparison. I felt so much pride just knowing that my brother was one of the most popular kids in school despite how different we were.

I received just as much attention because he was my brother. I tried to dress and talk like he did. Because my brother was known for being a good fighter and part of the football team, he was feared by the other kids as much as he was liked.

For a couple of years, I felt very close to my brother. I even was asked to be the waterboy for his football team. I had my team jersey and felt as if I was part of the team. Most of the time, my brother didn't pay much attention to me. I knew I was more of a burden to him but he still took me along with him everywhere he went.

I did not fit in with his friends because they were older than me. I wasn't as handsome or attractive as he was, and I was far from being an athlete. Though he didn't pay much attention to me, he was very protective of me. At times, his friends would pick on me, but he was quick to stop them.

When my brother told my mother that it was not his responsibility to take care of her kids, I felt a deep sense of disappointment in him. I admired and looked up to him! I had expected him to be more of a role model and protector with my siblings as he was with me. It was at that moment when we started to drift apart. He ventured off on his own, and eventually fell in love and began spending his free time with his girlfriend.

I was happy being part of the football team. I was happy being around my brother's friends, (even though they were not my friends directly), but I felt happy nonetheless. After my brother and I drifted apart, I started to feel bitter. I was happy being a part of my brother's life. I did not understand that I was living his life and not my own. I tried so hard to have his life that, I failed to find my own identity.

For the first time, I felt the feeling of rejection and abandonment. I did not have much of a relationship with my two younger brothers. I was spending so much time with my older brother that my two younger siblings were growing up on their own. As my brother and I drifted apart, a part of me died. I no longer felt like a happy kid. I started to act more of a parental figure to my two younger brothers than an older brother.

I started to become the protector of the family. Having received little to no affection from my mother, the only type of affection I was able to show to my younger brothers was that of a protector. I would protect my siblings just as my older brother did with me. I made sure that no one messed with them. I was a small kid, but I was very aggressive when it came to protecting my siblings. I learned how to fight from my older brother. Unable of showing affection to my siblings, the only way I could show my love was through protection.

The part of town where we lived was given the name "Rock Town" because of the high amounts of crack cocaine that was sold in the area. The population was predominantly Black American. White Americans were not allowed in our part of town. The brother who follows me was often taken for a white American and it was difficult for him to go to school without getting bullied. He was never taken serious when he tried to defend himself as being a "Latino." I loved him and I protected him the most, I was constantly engaging in physical altercations on his behalf. I would get into so many fights to intervene on his behalf that it became overwhelming!

My brother had no lack of self-control when it came to his tongue. He did not know how to just stay quiet when they were taunting him. I would countlessly tell him to just stay quiet and walk away or come and find me. He would not.

My younger brother was physically bigger than me but he was not as aggressive. I would constantly warn him, if he got into a fight and I had to get involved, the next person receiving punches would be him. I cannot remember how many fights I was involved in because of him.

No matter how many times I warned him, he would always find a way to get into trouble. I wonder if he provoked those boys on purpose because he knew that I would always be there do defend him! Maybe he felt that he needed someone close to him and it was his way of feeling loved.

I never feared getting into a fight; my fear was getting into trouble because I was the one who took care of everyone. My mother depended so much on me that I had to be careful making mistakes that would restrict me from helping my mom. I had a dual responsibility: I had to be responsible for my mom on the one hand, and on the other, I had to be a protector to my siblings.

There is no describing my youngest brother. He was fearless. He was about my size, but with no filter. He was not afraid of fighting; he was able to defend himself. I never feared him getting into fights as much as I feared him getting lost. He would roam the neighborhood all night with his friends. Some nights he would not come home... He was a nut-case on his own.

My older brother had gotten used to having me around him that he felt an absence when I chose not to follow him anymore. It would frustrate him having me around but yet he needed someone close to him. After I had made a decision to stay home and care for my siblings, he began taking our younger brother with him.

At the age of twelve, my older brother started taking him to parties and hangouts with his friends. He began introducing our youngest brother to drugs and alcohol. Our younger brother became more aggressive than the three of us. My younger brother became obsessed with being just as wild and daring as our oldest brother and took everything to the extreme.

There was no way of controlling his behavior. He drank what was offered and did every drug that was at his disposal. In one season of his life, he had started huffing. He would intentionally inhaled gasoline (or any other petrol distillate) to get high. Larger quantities with produce a euphoric effect and he loved it.

He would find any sort of aerosol spray, gas can, or whip cream bottle to get a quick high. One night, I received a call from one of his friends asking us to please go and pick him up at a nearby gas station, because he would not get his mouth off the gas pump.

The brother that follows me in line has always been calm in nature. He was the clown of the family and has a way of making everyone laugh. He has always been the glue that held everyone together. He was the only one who was very affectionate with my mother and my siblings. He had made friends with a bad crowd and got himself in trouble, but he was never a bad kid. The four of us were not easy on our mom. I do not know how my mom survived four boys like us! My older brother was careless, I was the serious one, and my youngest was wild. She did the best she could with us!

I have three sisters and yet I find it difficult to understand them. Because there is such a large age gap between us, they often seem like strangers to me. The oldest of my sisters is six years younger than me and the baby of the family is eleven years younger. I had moved out when my oldest sister was nine.

They grew up without me being a presence in their lives. I moved out when my eldest sister was nine. At gatherings, my sister's crowd around each other telling stories of things they used to do when they were younger, and I sit and wonder: "Where was I during all that time?" I enjoy knowing that they did not have to pass through the same difficulties as the boys did.

At the age of seventeen, I just became so weary dealing with so much dysfunction in my family that I decided to go and live with my grandmother. My mother was starting to date and I could notice how all of the dysfunction had a burden on her as well. It was more of the same dysfunction with my grandmother but I didn't have the burden to care for anyone.

My grandmother had been an alcoholic since the age of twenty-five and had many battles of her own. My uncle, the mechanic, had always been by her side. He inherited her battles of alcoholism. He always felt obligated to take care of her. My uncle and I shared the same room at my grandmothers but I didn't mind. Most days, it felt like it was my own room. He would usually pass out drunk outside in the car or would not come home at all.

A few months later, one of my grandmother's nephews came to live there as well. He was an older version of my youngest brother. He had amongst other addictions, an addiction to prostitutes. He left his home trying to start a new life but found himself being sucked into the same life he was trying to escape. I could not escape all the dysfunction. Everywhere I went, I was met with substantial instability.

One day, my grandmother called me into her room and asked me to return home to my mother. She explained to me that my mother depended so much on me, and I needed to be there for her and my siblings. My grandmother loved me more than all of her grandchildren. She gave me all the attention I could ever want. I did not understand why she would ask me to leave.

I did not have to fight for clothes and I had my own privacy for the first time in my life. My second cousin always slept on the couch. It was dysfunctional living with all the alcoholics in the house, but I had my own space. I did not want to go back home.

At the request of my grandmother, I moved back in with my mother. I do not know if my mother had some influence over my grandmother, but I never questioned her. I loved my grandmother and obeyed her. I moved back with my mother for a few more months helping her. She was having a difficult time with my sisters and needed me to help her.

My prayer for years was that my mother would find a nice man whom she could share her life with! I always felt that if she did not find someone to marry, I would follow my uncle's footsteps who felt an obligation for caring for my grandmother and living a life of bitterness.

She eventually found a nice gentleman who fell in love with her and accepted her with her seven kids. When she started dating him, my brothers had moved out and she only had my sisters. I was living with my grandmother, but moved back for a short time.

The first chance my mom told me they were getting married and he was going to move in, I did not think twice and packed my bags, found an apartment, and moved out. I thought for the first time, I would be on my own. That was short lived, my two younger brothers moved in with me a few weeks later.

My mother, for the first time in her life was discovering what married life was. I was struggling trying to find my identity. It was a new journey for my mother and me. We were both trying to adjust to a life that was completely new.

Her husband is a very affectionate man who treated her beyond what she could ask for. She did not know how to respond to him, because she only experienced abusive men in her life. I was struggling with my self-confidence. We had gotten so used to all the dysfunction that we felt out of place!

Just before my mother met my stepfather and married him, I had an encounter with Jesus and I gave my life to Him. I began serving in the church and later, became an ordained minister. Life seemed to be working out well for the both of us, but something did not feel right. As much as my mother and I tried to adapt to our new changes, we needed something to remind us of our dysfunctions. I allowed my two younger brothers to move in with me, because I needed the dysfunction to be present. Mom remained indifferent with her husband because she didn't know how to express her love to him. I knew deep inside that there had to be more than all the dysfunction in my life, but I didn't know how to get away from it. I struggled for years wondering if this is how my life was supposed to always be. Was I brought into this world to continue the cycle of dysfunction or was there more for me?

Chapter 2

My First Encounter with Church and Family Life

As a child, my grandmother would always remind me to smile and try to be happy. She said there was no need for me to walk around this world being so serious. My grandmother always knew that I carried a lot of my mom's burdens on my shoulders. She was always able to see things that made me wonder. Though she was an alcoholic, she would always remind me that it was not always the beer talking.

I didn't have many friends who I could relate to in school. Most of the kids at school were too busy being kids and enjoying life. I did not have the luxury of having fun, going out, or having a late-night sleep-over with friends. I felt I had the responsibility of attending to the needs of my siblings.

I met this kid from a mutual friend in school that was around my age. I had seen him around school and he would hang around some of the same friends, but I did not know him directly. He was good friends with my friend.

At first, he did not strike me as a kid with whom I would want to hang out with. He was only a couple of months older than me and physically he was a lot bigger than me. I did not like him too much because he would tend to take his jokes a bit too far! At times, because he was bigger than me, he felt that he was able to bully me around.

A couple of months before we became friends, we were with a group of kids from school and he took the joking way too far, almost like he was targeting me. It made me upset and almost pushed me to want to take it to the physical level, but I decided just to walk away. Because he was also my friends' friend, he would usually be at my friend's house hanging out. I decided not to visit my friend, if I knew this kid would be around.

One day, as I went to visit my friend, this kid was waiting outside his house. He told me that he was not home, and he had been waiting for him to come home. He had been waiting for about an hour outside of his home!

I said: "Ok". And presided to walk back home. The kid asked me, what I was doing today. I replied that I was bored so I figured I would come and hang-out. He stated he was bored as well. I turned around and started to walk back home, when he asked me if I wanted to hang with him. For a split second, I thought twice about hanging out with him, because of my previous experience. I didn't want to be rude so I turned towards him and asked him: "What did he have in mind? He said he didn't know!

I asked him if he wanted, he can come back home with me and we can play some video games. He said he wasn't into video games, but he liked to play basketball. I said: "Sure, let's go and play some ball". We hung out that day and I got to know him a little bit better outside of a social crowd. He was kind of cool!

Our mutual friend eventually moved and it was just him and I. It turned out; this kid didn't have many friends either. We were his only friends. For a short time, the three of us were inseparable! After our friend had moved, we started to hang out more, just the two of us.

I cannot remember if he was a bad influence on me or, if it was an agreement between us to get into trouble; but we would get into a lot of trouble. It could have been that we were just kids being kids. The more I got to know him, the more I was able to find that he was no different than me!

I thought that he had a perfect life. But it turns out; he was just as messed up as I was. I was starting to find someone whom I could relate to, and he felt the same towards me. The more we hung out, the more I realized that he was escaping his dysfunctions through the trouble we would get into. I started getting into fights in school and would constantly get suspended from school.

One day, he told me that his friend from Minnesota was in town visiting for a few weeks. He wanted to skip class and go and visit him, because he knew that his mother would not allow him to go after school. He asked me if I would go with him to visit his friend. I didn't like school too much, so I said "Ok!"

As we left school and started to walk, a police officer stopped us. I told my friend that we needed to run! but he was scared and said "no!" The police officer called us towards his patrol car. We decided to just stay and see what he had to say. He asked us where we were going. We told him that we were going home. The police officer said to us that he would give us a ride. I had a strange feeling that was not going to happen. The Police office took us to the police station on truancy!

Our parents were called to come and pick us up. The police officer at the station separated us so that we would not talk to each other while we waited for our parents to pick us up. My mom arrived first. She signed the papers and we left. In the parking lot, something inside of me told me to sit in the back seat, but I did not listen to that voice and sat in the front.

My mother is a small woman. She turned to me and smacked me across the chest as hard as she could. I got really upset and I yelled at her: "Why did you hit me? She was upset that she had to leave work early to come and pick me up. She started to yell at me about how my behavior was irresponsible!

Her hitting me did not upset me as much as the words she was telling me. She did not know of my struggles. I never had a close relationship with my mother. She did not know what I was going through in life or how I was feeling. She failed to realize that I was miserable. I wanted to yell out to her the same words that my older brother had said to her: "It's not my responsibility to take care of your kids!"

She did not know my frustrations! I was a kid forced to be an adult and she had the nerve to smack me. She did not know how my younger siblings at times did not want to listen to my instructions as I cared for them. One day, in my frustration trying to get my sister to take a shower, I punched the wall and left a hole in it. My mother saw the hole and was upset about it, but never questioned how it happened.

She did not know that I did not want to be in school anymore because of how ashamed I felt being poor. I could not dress like the other kids with the name brand shoes and clothes. I was not able to go to school with money to pay for a school dance or, buy snacks for fundraising. I had no confidence in myself to approach girls in my school that I liked. I liked school and I was pretty good at it, but my poor self-esteem did not allow me to enjoy it. My grades and school work were good I just didn't want to be in school.

As we drove home, she proceeded to tell me that ever since I started hanging out with this kid my attitude changed. I was becoming irresponsible according to her. Today, I look back and I realize that I was a kid; I was just acting like a normal kid. She told me that I could no longer hang around this kid because he was a bad influence over me.

My friend's mother showed up shortly after we had left. According to my friend, he did not get any type of physical punishment. His parents were Christians. They assisted a Pentecostal faith-based church. Instead of a physical punishment, his mother started to tell him how irresponsible he was being towards God and the church. She pointed out to him that I was a young man in need of God and he was failing to lead me to Him.

Instead of being a positive influence in my life, he was allowing himself to be influenced by me to do bad things. I do not know if his mother knew that we were going to visit his friend, and it was his idea to leave school but, in her eyes, I was a bad influence on her son.

His mother told him that he was no longer allowed to be friends with me. It turned out that the church where they assisted was a small Latino church with around twenty or thirty members of which only six of the members were youth. Two of the youth were nine and ten years old. The other young man in the youth group was eighteen and did not feel he was part of the youth group, and the other two were his sisters.

My friend was starving to have friends who he could relate too. He was dealing with his dysfunctions. His father did not attend church. He was battling with alcohol. He was a responsible hard-working man but was never much of a father to him. His father worked as a welder and provided a good income for the family. Between his mom's income and his father's, they were financially comfortable yet, I never figured out why with both of his parents working, they still lived in the bad part of town.

His father would buy a six-pack of beer a day and on the weekends he would buy a twelve-pack of beer for each Saturday and Sunday. Even though his father was battling with alcohol, I envied him for having his father present. He drank every day, but was not abusive or violent.

Though his father was present in his life, he would never do father-son activities as I would see on sitcoms. He would take him fishing now and then but it was just an excuse for him to drink more, play his music louder, and avoid his wife nagging at him to come inside because it was late. Even with all of that, I still envied him for at least knowing his father.

The following day at school, after getting in trouble with the truancy officer, he told me that he was no longer able to hang out with me. We both lost the only friend we had. We stopped hanging out for a few weeks. He started getting involved with the church. I figured I would go back to the routine of taking care of my siblings. Not much would have changed.

After a few weeks of not hanging out, I ran into him in the hallway at school. We started to talk and laugh about some of the trouble we had gotten into. We were both still without friends. He told me he was glad to have run into me because he was thinking about a plan that would allow us to hang out. He said to me: "What if you start coming to church with me? Maybe then my mom would see that you are a good kid and we can stay friends". We thought it was a great plan!

Church was not what I had in mind, but I said: "ok!" I had no desire of going to church. I liked to sleep in on Sunday mornings. On the weekends, my mom would take my younger siblings to the flea market and it would give me the chance to sleep with peace and quiet. The main reason that I said yes was simple: his sister was beautiful! She was older than me and I didn't think I had a chance with her, but it was worth a shot. The least that could happen is that I could sit close to her. That would be worth waking up early. He talked to his mom and they agreed to take me to church with them.

The church they attended was a very traditional Spanish Pentecostal church. I visited several churches when I was younger. In the part of town where I lived, there was a large Baptist church that would go to several neighborhoods in an old school bus picking kids up and would take them to church for the day. My mom would send us every Sunday.

At the time, I thought that she was concerned with our salvation. It turned out; this was her way to get some quiet time. We would visit the church forcefully, but they would feed us and most times we would win prizes. I had never heard of a Pentecostal church before, it was not like the Baptist church. It was different!

My family was not very religious. My grandmother was Catholic and all of my aunts and uncles believed they were Catholics as well, but no one attended a church service. At the Baptist church, we did not take it seriously. We would often get into fights with other kids from other neighborhoods. Other than the food and prizes, I did not want to be there.

I do not know how to describe visiting the church with my friend's family. It was different! I had no idea what to expect and felt nervous. First off, I did not have any dress clothes to wear; and second, it was a full Spanish church. Though we were Latinos, our family did not speak Spanish. I did not understand what the preacher was saying.

The only clothes I felt decent enough to wear were my white emoji shirt and a pair of worn blue jeans that I would try to save for special occasions! I felt embarrassed to go dressed in those clothes. I tried to make an excuse and get out of going, but my friend told me not to worry. He let me borrow a dress shirt. He was a lot bigger than me, so his shirt was two sizes larger. Even though the shirt fit large on me, it made me feel comfortable. I put the shirt on and off we went.

I knew a few words in Spanish, but I could not understand a full conversation. I did not understand a word the preacher was saying. The family would first attend Sunday school and then stay for the Sunday Service. I enjoyed the Sunday school class because the teacher spoke in English! It was a small group of youth: my friend and his two sisters, and the two younger brothers. The teacher spoke in a way to which we could relate.

I would sit in the class trying not to focus on my friend's sister but... at the same time trying to make her know of my interest in church. Other than her, I had no other interest in going. Not even the thought of continuing to hang out with my friend felt worth it. I didn't feel like I fit in.

I visited for several months with no effect. There was no fooling his mom. Our habits of getting into trouble remained the same. Fighting and getting suspended from school continued. We just had that rebellious attitude in us. I think we both felt that school was not for us! We did not fit in, more so I than him. I knew school was important but I had no goals and no encouragement. I felt that I did not have a future! What was the point of going if I would eventually end up like the rest of my family?

His mother presented to us the possibility of going to work. It didn't take much to convince us. I talked with my mom about the opportunity. I thought she would be happy but she wasn't. I knew she always felt that I would be successful and she wanted me to stay in school. She tried to convince me to stay in school, but I pleaded to her that school was not in my best interest at the moment, and it would be more beneficial to go and work.

I know she wasn't in agreement but she took me to the courthouse, and we got the work permit. Going to work seemed like the best choice, we did not have the temptation of getting into trouble. Though we were busy working during the week, we still had the itch for getting into some trouble. We still managed to find ways of getting into trouble. My friend was learning how to drive his parent's car. On several nights, after his parents went to bed, we would take their car for joy rides and managed to get ourselves into trouble.

One day, his mother became upset with him over something we did at work. He tried to shift the blame on me, but his mother said something to him that left an impact on my life up to this day. She said to him: "Look at what you are doing; you say that he is your friend, yet you live your life carelessly. What if your friend died today, he would go straight to Hell and you would have that on your conscience for the rest of your life? Talk to him about God instead of leading him to trouble, he is a good kid but he needs God in his life".

I don't think it was much of her words about God and going to Hell that stunned me, it was her noticing that I was not a bad kid. She knew that it was her son doing all the mischievous things and would drag me along. At that moment, for the first time in years, I felt good about myself.

My mother never told me how proud she was of me or how much she appreciated all the work I was doing, caring for my siblings while she was working. I always felt that my mother was proud of me but, she never let me know if it! She never encouraged me to be successful! Hearing those words from my friend's mother made me feel that someone cared about me.

Hearing those words shifted something inside of me; I started to see something different in them. Not so much in my friend but in his mom and even in his dad. It seemed that nothing would change him. The more time I spent with them, the more I started to notice that even with all their dysfunctions, they were a family.

They would go to the grocery store together. Everyone would throw things in the shopping cart without question. Sundays after church, they would all go out to eat as a family. Now and then, the dad would go to church. On the days he wouldn't go, they would go home and pick him up. He would be half-way through his twelve-pack of beer, but they would still go and eat as a family.

They would set time before the end of the day to read a few Bible verses and pray together. They had their typical family problems. Many were noticeable and there were many hidden secrets. I started to overlook all of their problems, because I was seeing all the good in them.

I cannot compare them to the sitcom families but they showed me – for the first time – what a real family looked like. As bad as his father was, he was still a presence in the life of his son. It was enough to make me envious of him. His mother was extremely religious, but it was ok! My friend had been addicted to pornography at a very young age and managed to hide his secret.

His sisters were desperate to turn eighteen and leave the house. The father, he was strange, but he was a hard-working family man. They had their dysfunctions but they were a family. Far better than anything I had ever had. It was at that moment when I said to myself that I wanted what they had! I did not want all the dysfunction they were dealing with, but I wanted to have a family like theirs.

I started to spend more time with them. At my friend's mother's request, he would often talk to me about the Bible, but he would just only focus on the book of Revelations and practically scared me to death. It was this fear of going to Hell which prompted me to accept Jesus as my Lord and Savior. I still had no interest in church but I didn't want to go to Hell!

I would spend so much time with them that I forgot I had a family of my own. The times I would go home to see my mother and siblings, I would try to get them to eat together or get everyone together to talk, but wasn't successful. Because I was spending more time with my friend and his family, my siblings often saw me as a traitor. I would get this feeling that they felt I had abandoned them!

It was a strange feeling. Even though I was spending less time at home, I would help my mother financially. She no longer needed to work long hours. She was spending more time at home which allowed me to spend time at my friend's. They had come to accept me and almost adopted me.

At the age of sixteen, the company my mother worked for decided to move its operations to Virginia. She worked for the company for several years. They offered her a promotion with a pay increase if she would move with them. She felt it would be a good change, so she decided to take the position and moved. I did not want to go!

I was working and was doing ok. I felt that I could become independent. I told her that I would not be going with her. She was ok with my decision. I figured I could bounce back and forth from my friend's house and my grandmother's house. I had been staying out of trouble and my mother knew I was doing well for myself!

To my surprise, around the same time as my mother was moving to Virginia, my friend's family was contemplating moving to Iowa. The family dearly loved the Pastor that founded the church and decided to follow him to Iowa. The pastor felt a calling to move and start a church in Iowa a few years prior to me visiting the church. They had been praying about going to Iowa and heling build the church. They offered me to go with them! This would be a drastic change for me! I was unsure of what I wanted to do. I loved my job and it was going well. I was starting to get used to the church. I did not get a good feeling of moving with them. I was receiving Bible studies from the youth minister, because of my decision to give my life to Christ. I was a few months away from getting baptized in the name of Jesus. Everything was going so well then from one day to the next, it all seemed to be falling apart so quickly.

Within weeks, my mother had moved to Virginia and my friend's family had moved to Iowa. I decided not to go with either. I stayed and lived with my grandmother. I figured I would manage and find a way to continue working and going to church.

In a matter of weeks, everything had come to an end. I did not drive, and I didn't have a car. I lost my job because I could not get there. The church was also going through a transitional period after having lost the pastor. The church moved from its location because of financial struggles. The youth pastor decided to take a ministerial leave and the current Pastor was losing the church because of conflicts within the congregation and divisions. Everything that I had come to enjoy… was coming to a dead end!

Chapter 3

Reflection on My Life

Spending time with my friend and his family, made me realize how dysfunctional my family was! I knew everyone had problems and up to a certain point, I felt that our family was not that bad compared to others. I had a friend whose father had his own flooring company and they were living well. My friend always dressed nicely and had nice things.

His family had one of the biggest homes in the neighborhood. Yet, his parents were married but each had open relationships with other people. They had chosen not to get divorced or move out until my friend was old enough to choose with which parent he wanted to live with.

Another friend of mine had an abusive father who was constantly beating his mother. She had to cater to his father's every demand, or else, she would be beaten. His father had a lawn business and on weekends, my friend would have to go to work with him. His father never gave him, or his mother, any money. He not only was an abusive father, but he was also an aggressive alcoholic.

Even though my family had our dysfunctions, my mother did her best to raise us. She was working within her physical and social means to ensure our needs were being met. Though we wore the same clothes repetitively, she always made sure we had clean clothes. Our emotional needs were an area that my mother struggled with, mainly, because this was also passed down from her mother and father. My mother always struggled to express her emotions towards us.

In our family, it was rare to hear: "I love you." We never had family reunions. When all of my aunts and uncles did get together, it meant there was some sort of family crisis! It was not uncommon to know that my mother was not talking to one of her sisters or my grandmother or my grandmother to one of her kids. There was always some reason as to why our families did not come together. If, by chance, someone was able to manage to get everyone together, the night would usually end with someone offended or offending someone.

My grandmother loved me so much! I have always been her favorite amongst her more than twenty grandchildren. Since before I was born, she knew that I would be someone great in this world. I do not know much about her childhood. I would ask her questions about her life as a young girl, and she would always tell me stories of her struggles.

She had a difficult childhood. She is the type of person that carries everyone's burdens on her shoulders. All her pain and struggles in life led her to be filled with a lot of resentment and bitterness and her alcoholism didn't help. Yet, even though she has had her struggles, she is one of the most loving persons you would ever meet.

I do not know too much about my grandfather. I met him – a few years back – and spent some time with him as we worked together; but he was always very distant. My aunts and uncles held a lot of resentment towards him. I would ask my mom and grandmother questions about him but I was often met with silence.

Often my grandmother would look at me with anger and tell me: "You look just like your grandfather." She would express her anger she felt towards him through her words to me. He had fallen in love with my grandmother's sister but He was forced by his parents to marry my grandmother, because they felt it was more convenient for him. He didn't love her yet felt obligated to marry her.

Eight children later, my grandfather felt that he no longer wanted to be in a family he did not want. He brought the family to Florida from Michigan, and abandoned the family. This opened the door for a lifetime of bitterness and anger in my family that would transcend into the next generation. The feeling of abandonment, rejection, and anger towards him, led my grandmother and uncles to alcoholism and my aunts to enter into abusive relationships.

My grandmother had made her peace with Jesus – decades later – but it would be short-lived. She was never able to forgive and allow herself to be free from the bitterness. Though she loves the

Lord and is always praying for everyone, she carries so much pain in her heart.

The eldest daughter (my first aunt) had left the house at the first chance. She met a man whom she felt loved her and was going to take her away from all of the pain, only to have the bitterness follow her. Her husband took her and their children to California because he did not want her to have any contact with her family. It would be decades later that my mother was able to make contact with her. We moved to California and stayed with the family for a short period. There was no hiding how much the resentment had created so much dysfunction in her family.

My mother (who was the second oldest) also had her run-in with a man who would eventually leave her with two boys. She would go one to have seven children being a single mother for years. She had her share of abusive men coming in and out of her life and her children battling with the same plague of resentment that had hindered my grandmother and her eight children.

My first and oldest uncle, who always lived by my grandmother's side, inherited her bitterness and resentment leading to alcoholism. My second uncle thought he was a gigolo and had every addiction in life except work. My third uncle is doing life in prison on murder charges and the youngest of my four uncles, has had his struggles, has manage to do well. My aunts have all struggled with their share of failed marriages, alcoholism, and their children victims of sexual abuse and abandonment. Despite their difficulties, my aunts have done far better than my uncles, but you can still sense the pain in them.

I would question my grandmother about her parents trying to understand our family history. She would not talk much about her life and parents, but I was able to get a few details from her. Her father was a very harsh man. He was also very abusive to his wife and children. Her mother had twelve children! My grandmother did not want to get married but was forced to and became pregnant at the age of sixteen. She knew always knew that my grandfather had loved her sister. She had eight children: four boys and four girls.

All of the pain, resentment, and bitterness had been passed down from one generation to the next. The third generation, which involves my siblings and me, were victims of what was passed down to us. I do not believe that any one of my siblings or cousins are aware of the depth of our roots of pain and suffering. It was common to see my aunts and uncles in and out of different relationships. They battled with instability for years. One of the worst battles a family can encounter is that of abandonment and rejection. It took years for most of them to recover. Eventually, my aunts and one uncle have been in a stable marriage that has lasted years.

There was no escaping the reality of my life: poverty, lack of formal education, lack of emotional support, and lack of direction or guidance in life. The only encouragement I would receive from my uncles – and now – from my older brother who had succumbed to the plague that consumed my aunts and uncles was that: "It was my destiny to follow in their footsteps".

I would constantly be reminded of how alcoholism ran through my veins. Alcohol was a daily part of my surroundings. I never understood how there was never money to pay the bills or to buy groceries, but there was always money for beer!

My mother and my friend's family eventually moved. My decision to stay with my grandmother proved to be one of the worst decisions that I could have made. There is a saying that says: "If you can't beat them, join them". It seemed almost inevitable. All of my positive influences had left. Though my mother never was able to express encouraging words to me, I always felt that she held me to a higher standard than my siblings or cousins.

Maybe she always knew that there was something different about me. However, with her living in Virginia, I did not have her presence to remind me that "I was a responsible, hard-working young man!" I could not explain all that was happening to me. It had fallen apart so suddenly. I had no job, no way of getting to church (even if I did go to church), and there wasn't anyone to whom I could relate. The youth minister took leave from the ministry and took with him the English Sunday school. I was stuck in a bad place. I felt useless!

My grandmother was happy to receive me. She made sure I had everything I needed and did her best to spoil me. During the day, it was quiet. My grandmother would usually spend her mornings cooking, washing clothes and cleaning. She would find ways to cook a meal out of nothing. I never had to worry about not having anything clean to wear. My two pants and two shirts were always cleaned and pressed. The evenings were the scary part of my days.

"Fwshhhhh…" The sound of the first beer being opened at 5 pm. To some, the sound of a beer can opening signifies that it's time to start the party! For me, it signified that it was time to run! I don't mean that lightly.

As the night progressed and the beers began to be emptied, one by one, the music and their voices would become louder. My grandmother would have the beers out in a cooler waiting for my uncles or her husband to get home. The beers would be nice and cold waiting for them.

The drinking would go on until midnight. My grandmother would then start to kick everyone to bed so they could be rested for work the next day. Most nights, the party ended with the last beer being drunk. If my uncle who smoked marijuana would be there, it was constantly every hour going to the back of the house to smoke. There was never any shortage of drugs or alcohol in the house.

Four out of the seven days consisted of heavy drinking. Mondays were a calm evening. Someone was usually hung-over and needed to rest. Wednesday was also a rest day, and Thursday there was no money. I didn't drink or smoke at the time, so I was the designated DJ. It was my job to make sure the right music was playing. It kept me busy for a while and away from the temptation of drinking. I could not play music that would make anyone violent; I had to stay away from love songs, because someone would start to cry; absolutely no hip-hop or new-age music was allowed; the music had to be drinking music. It was a very toxic environment so much that anyone who came in was contaminated. I was just a ticking time-bomb waiting to explode.

As the days went by, I was being exposed to more and more of what had consumed my family for generations, bitterness, anger, and resentment. Day by day, my uncle would invite me to the back to smoke. Another uncle would offer me a beer. My brother would constantly tell me that I should just drink with them because it was a matter of time, before I was going to be like them. As the days went by, the more I felt I was in a losing battle.

There were a few rules in place: if you opened a beer or lit a cigarette, you better finish it. If someone would get violent, they had to leave immediately. There was absolutely no crying allowed, and no one ever came empty-handed (beer, cigarettes, or drugs). Everyone who came to the house thought it was the coolest place on earth. It was a hangout for so many people.

The first couple of weeks living at my grandmother's house were ok. I felt strong enough to resist. I still believed that I gave my life to Jesus and I needed to keep myself focused on my spiritual life. As the weeks passed by, the temptation grew stronger and stronger. Eventually, I did not have the strength in me to resist. I gave into what I did not want to be a part of.

One drink leads to two. A puff leads to having my own marijuana cigarette. Little by little all the desires of having a sitcom family started to fade away. I believed deep inside that I was destined to break the generational curse that had plagued our family for generations. I believed that I could one day have a family of my own, and be able to do the things that I would see the television families do. Who was I kidding? What I wanted to get away from was always present!

I was getting close to turning seventeen and I had not had a girlfriend. There were a few girls in school that I liked but... I never had the nerve to go and talk to them. I liked my friend's sister. The more time I spent around her, the more I thought I was getting her to like me, (at least I thought). She had started to open up to me before they moved.

She had stopped going to school when she was twelve. Even though I stopped going to school at the age of fourteen, I was knowledgeable. She would constantly be studying for the GED test on her own, and would ask me for help. She knew I was smart and could help her. I enjoyed spending time with her as her tutor. But it never went further than that. They moved away and I lost contact with the family.

Every night I hung around my uncles; I would always be taunted by them. They would tell me that they were going to bring me a prostitute to show me how to be a man. One night, my uncles decided they were going to go and get some prostitutes. I knew I was inexperienced with girls but this was not what I had in mind, much less my idea of the father-son conversation about girls. Had it not been for a friend who asked me to walk him home, I would have been thrown into the arms of a prostitute.

I drank a few beers just for fun when I was younger, but there is no comparison in drinking for fun and drinking out of anger and bitterness. I eventually gave in to the temptation to drink a beer. Drinking that night gave me the worst feeling I had ever felt. I was not drinking for fun; it was out of anger. I was angry because this was not how my life was supposed to be! I felt there was more to my life than this. I was angry because no matter how hard I had tried to change my future; something was dragging me back. I did not know how to escape the generational curse let alone know that a generational curse existed!

As I started to drink, I started to have a lot of questions run through my mind. Was spending more time with my friend and his family, my way of escaping what my reality was, or was it possible that my life could change? Did I create a fantasy life by watching all of those sitcoms? If I accepted Jesus in my life, why was my life being torn apart? With all the questions, I finally realized that the idea of having a wonderful marriage and family would never happen to me.

With all my questions and no answers, the anger inside of me just grew. After brushing off all of those thoughts, I said to myself: "I just don't care anymore!" If this was the life I was destined to live, then I was going to live it without care! I wasn't working and I did not have any money. I didn't have much to do during the day and started to feel lazy. I was bored one day and I decided to go for a walk. I ran into some of the guys that I knew from school. I had been out of school for a couple of years, so I was surprised that these guys remembered who I was.

They remembered me because of all the fights I would get into. I would get into so many fights, yet I never got beat up. They asked me if I wanted to hang out with them. I didn't have much going on so I said "Ok!" I went to their hangout. It turned out to be a gang house.

The fights I would get into were to protect my brothers but never out of malice. They remembered how good a fighter I was and asked me if I wanted to join their gang. This gang was not like the one my older brother had been involved with. They were more aggressive and had already built a reputation for being involved in several murders. I found a place where I could fit right in. A bunch of young Latino men with no ambition, no drive, no future, and no hopes of escape. I tried to fit in with them as much as I could, but it didn't feel right. The more you are around certain people, the more their influence brings about changes in you. I chose to stay in the gang house for days, and began to enjoy going out late at night to do whatever would get us money. I started to do more drugs with them. Their influence and drugs caused me to become more violent. The fights I would get into while with them were fights not for survival but destructive. We would steal or rob people to feed our drug habits. We did not care we hurt or stole from.

Eventually, I started selling drugs. Being part of a gang meant that you had to pay dues. The leader would set a quota for each member. At every meeting, every member either had to present cash or something of value that could be sold. This money was invested in buying drugs, weapons, and cars for the gang and there was no negotiating the quota.

You either brought the money or had to pay a fine which consisted of a beating. There was no option: either you sold drugs or you would steal valuable goods. The young man that was once a responsible hard-worker, who took care of his family, and accepted Jesus into his life was slowly fading away. I could not even recognize who I had become.

I had always been a resourceful individual. I had gotten a reputation for being the go-to guy. If you needed something, I would be the person to approach. If I did not have what you were looking for, I would find ways of getting it, or find someone who was able to get it. Whenever there was a drought of marijuana or cocaine, I would be the person who could find it. I was highly sought after. I was so busy building my reputation that I would forget about my grandmother and my mom.

I would call my mother to check up on her every now and then. Some weeks would go by when my grandmother would not hear from me – I was too busy doing my own things. One day, my grandmother woke me up for breakfast around noon-time. As I ate, she asked me if I had called my mother. I told her I had not spoken to her in several days.

She told me that my mother had been asking her if I would like to go up to Virginia with her. I do not know if my grandmother told her of the mess, I had gotten myself into. I told my grandmother: No, I was ok!

She then asked me if I would consider going up to Virginia and help her. It seemed strange that my grandmother was asking me these questions. For the first time, I felt I was free. I felt that I was doing what I wanted and what I was destined to do. I did not want to go back to taking care of my siblings. I did not want to be responsible for anyone. I don't think I even cared about myself.

If my life was meant to be so dysfunctional then I was going to live it to the fullest – a life that would lead me to end up just as bitter and angry as my uncles. This was the life I was destined to live — a life drowning in my misery. Maybe someday, I would find someone, fall in love, have some kids, and then ruin it. I would be a biological father to kids I would never see or love. That was the path that made more sense to me.

For weeks, my grandmother insisted that I go and help my mother. I would call my mom on the phone and she would ask me to go up and be with her. I tried avoiding her calls at times just to ignore the question. One day, after several weeks of insistence from my grandmother and my mother, I told my mom I would go for a week or two, and see what happens. I figured I would go, let her know that it wasn't working out, and come back home. I eventually moved to Virginia. I was taken out of the environment I was starting to enjoy, and going back to the environment that felt like a prison. I was not happy about the move, so I would remind myself that it was only temporary.

Virginia was nice. My mother was living in a small country town. For the first couple of weeks, I was detoxing and felt miserable. After things settled down, I felt bored so I found a part-time job. I was broke so I figured it would be ok for a while. I fell back into the routine of working, giving my mom my paycheck to help her with the bills, and taking care of my siblings. It was miserable because I had gotten so used to selling drugs, sleeping in, and having no responsibilities. Going back to work for such little money did not seem normal. It was a difficult transition. I eventually stuck it out for a few months. I was starting to get to know some of the guys from work and would hang out with them.

My mother stayed a few more months trying to make things work out, but she eventually decided to move back to Florida. I was upset when she told me that she wanted to move back home. I gave up everything to be here with her only for her to move back. I was angry. I had been clean and sober for a few months now. Feeling that anger once again drove me to want to get high or drunk. I had a few friends that would give me a ride to and from work. They would invite me to parties or just to hang out but I never joined them. After my mother told me she had decided to move back, I told her that I was going to stay. I found some friends that were going to rent me a room. I wanted to be happy and I wanted to be free. I believe my mother knew that she was losing me in the sense that I wanted to move on with my life and not be tied down caring for her and my siblings. She moved back to Florida and I put myself back in a place where my decision led me into a vulnerable position.

At work, I met this young lady who was not the type of girl that attracted me physically but she had a very nice personality. She had a daughter who was a year old. I do not know what her intentions were, but she was always nice to me. She would pick me up and drop me off from work. One day, she invited me to her parents' home to meet them. Her father was a police officer and was very nice. Her mother was a stay at home wife and was just as nice. They had a nice home out in the country. I had never been to such a nice home as theirs in all my life.

She had moved out of her parents' home because she had made some poor decisions and lost custody of her daughter. Her parents had custody of her daughter. She would visit her parents daily so that she could spend time with her daughter. She never wanted to go alone so she would always drag me with her. On some days, we would stay the night. The parents allowed me to sleep in their guest bedroom.

The term, "Guest Bedroom" was strange to me. I had always lived in places where at least three or four people shared one bedroom. If all the bedrooms were full, then you slept in the living room. The family treated me very well. They had had a son that was about my size that moved out and started his own family and was doing fairly well for himself.

They must have noticed that I did not have clothes, so they gave me all of their son's clothes. He had no plans of coming for them and the mother was looking for a reason to get rid of them. They were nice clothes so I didn't mind.

Every night for dinner, I was supposed to take a shower and come to dinner dressed almost to impress (well, at least, in my mind). The father would spend time with me talking to me about school. He was very encouraging but I could not understand why they were being nice to me. It was very noticeable that I lacked social etiquette because I looked and talked like a gang member so I don't know why her father would bother spending time with me.

He had a 1969 Plymouth that was a smaller version of a Dodge Charger sitting in his yard. Every day I would look at the car, open the door and hood or just sit inside. Her dad told me that he bought that car years ago to work on it with his son, but his son was never into classic cars. It was just sitting there rotting away. I guess he must have seen how my eyes would light-up seeing the car. One day he said to me, "You like that car, don't you?" I responded to him that it was a nice car. He then offered to sell it to me very cheap. I could not believe what he was telling me. He was practically giving it away to me. I could not believe how this family was treating me. I didn't understand why they clothed me and trusted me in their home. Had I been my old-self from a few months ago, I would have probably stolen what I could. They treated me as a family member and not like a gang member.

What I felt with my friend and his family back in Florida was nothing compared to this family. The dad did not drink. He liked to fix things. The mother was always cooking and cleaning. They spent a lot of time as a family. I could honestly compare them to a television series family. They were perfect. At least I thought they were. I'm sure they had their issues. I could not understand how their daughter turned out to be a mess. She was always very disrespectful towards them. She had the perfect parents, the perfect home, and a perfect life here with them, what would have driven her to make such poor choices in life?

One day, just when I thought things were going great, just as I started to think, "I can find a way to fall in love with this girl and become an official part of this family," she tells me to get my stuff because we were leaving. She completely caught me off guard.

Moments before, I was having a good conversation with her father. She had her daughter in one arm and with her free hand pulls me and directs me violently towards the door. Her mother comes rushing towards the door and starts yelling at her that she is not to take the baby out of this house. A yelling match takes place between them so much that the father had to step in. By that point, I decided to walk outside and leave them to it. I could hear everything from outside the house. From the outside, I heard her father yelling at her: "If you try leaving this house with the baby, I will arrest you for kidnapping!" I was just shaking my head. I couldn't believe what was happening. What could this girl possibly have done? For weeks things were going great.

A few moments later, in a fit of rage, she walks outside and tells me to get into the car; then, she brings me a trash-bag full of clothes that the family had given me, and we left. I did not get a chance to say goodbye to her parents. There went my chances of buying my first car.

With no place for us to go, I asked her if she could drop me off at my friend's house who rented me a room. She would bounce back and forth with some of her cousins. I had been spending so much time with her and her family, I had forgotten I had a place to stay. I had been down this road once before. I already knew that feeling of getting so attached and falling in love with something only to have it ripped out from me. She dropped me off and she drove off. She didn't say sorry, she didn't explain anything, and she didn't want to talk. The drive home was an awkward silence. She left and I carried on my normal routine of going to work and coming back home.

A few weeks later, she came knocking at the door around two in the morning. She smelled of alcohol and she looked like a mess. She asked if she could stay for the night. For a split second, I knew I should not have let her in, but I did. She had allowed me to stay with her family for a few weeks, so I figured I owed her.

During the time I spent with her, she was going through a phase of cleaning herself up so that she could regain custody of her daughter. Before I met her, she had lost custody of her daughter because of her drug habits. She was using me to fool her parents into thinking that she met a nice guy and would be cleaning up her act and making better choices in life. Once again, I was being used to fool someone's parents! I thought she really liked me.

She stayed with me for a couple of weeks, until I just got fed up with her. She did nothing but drink alcohol and get high. She would constantly ask me for money for beer or cigarettes. She was a few years older than me and, in a way, I liked her. I was not attracted to her physically, but before she let herself go, she was a nice person.

She was pretty, but her lifestyle hid a lot of her beauty. I had gotten to know a good side of her for a short time. The person that came out with the drugs and alcohol was a completely different person. One night, when she came home, it was clear she wanted to have sex for the first time with me. She was not herself! I knew what she wanted but because of my lack of self-confidence and experience, I became fearful and timid. It was not a fear of being intimate, but rather the fear of: "Not knowing what I am doing or having the experience she was wanting".

She started hugging me and tried to kiss me several times. Her kisses were not soft and sweet as I would have imagined it, they were aggressive. Her aggressiveness was not bothering me, what began to bother me was her taunting me for my inexperience and "her wanting to make me a man". She would laugh at how she would take my virginity away. Had she not started taunting me, I would have probably succumbed to the desires. I wanted to engage in intimacy with her…Why not? I was getting close to eighteen years old. I never had a girlfriend. Truth be told, I never even kissed a girl. Her touching me provoked me enough to engage with her.

As much as I tried to respond to her, I just could not get past the words she would use to taunt me. Had she expressed herself differently, I would have followed through with it. I finally pushed her away and asked her to stop. She kept trying to provoke me, and I finally asked her to get her stuff and leave. She picked up her stuff and in profanely dismal terms, told me I would die a virgin.

Once again, I was met with the feeling of disappointment. Who was I deceiving? I was not meant to be a family man. I was not husband material. It had been several months since I felt that anger and resentment as when I drank that beer at my grandmother's house. Once again, I was angry. It was late, and I did not have access to drugs or alcohol or else it would have been open season. There was only one thing left for me to do. The following day, I called my mom and let her know things were not working out here.

She didn't ask, and I didn't say much more. She said she would send my brother to come up and get me. I sent her money to give him and he came within a few days to pick me up

Chapter 4

My Life Turned Upside Down

I had spent several months living on my own in Virginia. It was challenging especially being seventeen. I made some good friends who helped me, but it was not easy relying on others. Back home, though I was spending a lot of time with my friend and his family, I knew that my mother and grandmother were close if I needed them. I felt safe just knowing they were close by.

Living on your own, far from family, there are no safety nets. My best option was to return home no matter how dysfunctional I thought it was. I would be turning eighteen soon. I was starting to realize that life is not how it appears to be on television.

There were many unhappy endings to my nights. My day did not end with a hug and a speech of how everything was going to be alright. My nights ended with much disappointment. Some nights, I would go to bed angry, others I would drown my sorrows in drugs or alcohol.

Could it be possible that one could achieve a great marriage and have a sitcom family? Was there such a thing of a perfect family or was that just a lie? The more I would question all my disappointments, I realized I was probably expecting too much. I was coming to terms with the idea that if there was such a thing (a happy marriage, kids, a nice home, and a perfect sitcom life), it was not meant for me.

I was not dealt a good hand. I was young but thrust into adulthood early in life. I was never taught that life could get better. Throughout my life, I was met with much adversity but the dream of a sitcom fantasy life still tugged at me. However, I did not want to live with my mother; she was struggling to find work and I did not want to be an extra mouth for her to feed so I decided I would stay with my grandmother.

I failed to realize that my mother had been working for years and being unemployed was making her depressed. I too was encountering depression. My mother needed my help and I abandoned her.

I was allowing the anger to overtake me. I had been sober for a couple of months now. My time in Virginia helped me to get out of the gang life involved with drugs and worse. I would occasionally drink and do drugs with my friends in Virginia but it was more on a social level. Working and spending time with my friend's parents kept me away from getting too involved with my friends.

Coming back home and being unemployed was starting to take its toll on me. I was never able to speak to my mother about the emotional changes that I was going through. I did not know how to open up to her. I always managed to keep everything bottled up inside of me. Going through the hormonal changes that a young man goes through was difficult. I did not know to whom to turn for guidance. I hated my life!

I never told my mother directly, but I would blame her for the misery that besieged me. I thought it was her fault that my life and the lives of my siblings were so miserable! Though it was not fair of me to blame her because she did the best she could, I felt it necessary to blame her for my misery.

I was curious about my biological father but did not have the courage to ask about him. I never knew the man…though; I met him once a few years later, it was too late for me to care. My older brother had reached out to him and tried to build a relationship with him. He would beg me to meet him. I would tell him in anger: "Where was he when I needed him in my life? I have done well for myself all of these years!" And I can continue doing so without him.

I refused to meet him. One day, my brother brought him to our house so he could meet me. I was outside cleaning my car when they came. I had no choice but to face him. I shook his hand and respectfully said: "It was nice to meet him!" He tried to make conversation with me, but there was not much for me to talk to him about. They left shortly after my brother became upset with me for being so cold to him. That was the last time I ever saw him. I felt my world was collapsing and I had no hope. I could not see a way out for me. I had been so in love with the idea of marriage that I could not let it go. In spite of the fact that there was nothing working in my favor to allow me to overcome my situation, I continued to fight the hopelessness that was engulfing me.

Perhaps, it was best just to give up on the idea and accept the life to which I was born. For the first month, I just stayed at my grandmother's house and would not go out. I would help her around the house to stay busy. She was not pressuring me to get a job or to do something with myself. There was nothing I could ever hide from my grandmother. She knew that I was struggling internally. She would tell me now and then: "Come on man, get up, and do something with your life!" At times, I felt it was the alcohol in her speaking. I was able to open up to her a bit, but I kept most of my issues to myself.

The routine at my grandmother's had not changed. It was a constant environment of drinking and drugs. I had managed to stay away from participating for a couple of weeks but as the days passed, it was becoming difficult to resist. I had been looking for work for several weeks but... was unsuccessful. The money that I had saved from Virginia was coming to an end. My options were running out. My work permit had expired and my options for work were limited. I did not want to work in a fast-food chain. I was starting to give up. It was a constant temptation to drink or do drugs at my grandmother's. The pressure would build up every day. One night, my brother handed me a beer. He said to me: "There's no escaping what you were meant to be!" I sat with the beer in my hand contemplating whether I should open it or not. That moment felt like an eternity! My life was flashing before my eyes. I had been in this position before and the choice I made led me down a dark path. I was not sure if I wanted to go down that path again. That cold beer started to warm up. At one point, someone said to me: "If you're not going to drink that, give it to me!" It snapped me out of the daze. There were rules to being at my grandmother's house I had to follow. If you get a beer, you better drink it. A voice inside of me said: "Accept what you are meant to be and drink the beer!"

In anger, I drank the beer. That voice in my head yelled out: "Yeah Boy, it's on now!" Whatever small hope inside me died in that instance. I did not care and I did not allow myself to think about marrying and having a family life. If my life was not meant to include marriage or have a family life, then I was not going to allow myself to fantasize about one. I began to live carelessly! There were days that I would wake up not knowing whose house I was in. I did not remember getting to where I was or how I got there. I didn't care if I lived or died! I didn't care who I hurt and I was determined not to allow myself to get hurt. No one could hurt me, there had been enough hurt already inside. It was just me against the world.

The money I had saved to buy the Plymouth that my friend's dad was selling was running out. I had six hundred dollars left and I could not buy a car for that much. Besides, I didn't have a driver's license so it didn't make sense to buy a car. I had to invest the money or I would spend it. I decided to invest it in a pound of marijuana.

Previously I had been dealing drugs. Most of that money that I made selling drugs was to pay my quota fees in the gang. Though I did not want to sell drugs, let alone get back involved with the gang, this seemed my only option. I had previously built up a good reputation, so finding clients would not be difficult. Selling drugs was not hard; the hard part was not consuming my profits — I could not allow myself to smoke what I had to sell. I had to be careful with my next plan of action: I would take half a pound to sell and the other half to consume. I would sell enough to make a profit and have enough left over to pay my bills, at the same time, yield enough for my personal use.

The cost of a pound of good grade marijuana in the '90s was less than six hundred dollars. I was able to sell a half-pound parceled out for eight hundred – it was an easy process. I was buying a pound and selling half a pound a week but consuming the unsold half the same week.

I would not sell on street corners as when I was involved with the gangs because my clients were working-class adults. There was no drama and the risk was minimal. By this time I had spent several months living carelessly and dealing drugs. I felt happy and important.

Towards the end of my binge, my uncle asked me if I wanted to work with him. The company he worked for received a large contract and they needed extra help. I was doing well enough not to have to work so I was not interested at first. Partying every night can become overwhelming. Waking up hung-over or dealing with people who had no money was frustrating. To be honest, I felt lazy. Working for a few weeks wouldn't be bad. I figured I would soon become bored with it and go back to partying.

The night job consisted of being on a molding machine pressing a button. It was not complicated or stressful, however, it was a fast-paced job. The mold machine would spit out the part and the button had to be pressed quickly so that the machine would not cool down. I enjoyed it! I was working an eight-hour shift in the evening. I was able to sleep in, spending my mornings relaxing and then going to work.

One evening, the owner of the company had a meeting with all of the night shift. He presented to everyone the opportunity of working twelve-hour shifts, seven days a week. My uncle loved the idea of working overtime. He asked me if I wanted to work those hours with him. I did not have much going on, besides, he was my ride. I would either have to quit or accept the hours. The night supervisor was only a few years older than me. His father-in-law was the owner of the company. He was a great person to work with. He knew that my uncle and I were pot-heads. Because of the twelve-hours that we were working, we did not get a lunch break.

The owner allowed us to have fifteen-minute break every two hours instead of the lunch break. The late-night hours were long. My uncle somehow convinced the supervisor to allow us to smoke outside. He allowed us to smoke pot at every break on the condition that we did not slack off at the job. This had been the best decision I had made in a few years! Where else would I find a job that allowed me to smoke on the job? It also benefited me as I picked up a lot of clients. My uncle met a lady who worked the day shift. They had been dating for several months before I started working. She mentioned to my uncle that her niece would be moving from Puerto Rico and was going to live with her with the hopes of working at the factory. She wanted to introduce her to me. My uncle mentioned this to me but I did not give it much thought. I was enjoying life. Everything seemed to be running smoothly at work with my side business so I did not want to get distracted by a girl. My uncle and his girlfriend found a way to get us to meet. My uncle would always stop at his girlfriend's house before work to smoke. He was my ride so I had no choice. I didn't mind it; she was a nice lady and, on some days, she would cook for us. One day, he was very insistent that we go to her house earlier than usual. Some days, they would lock themselves in the room and I would wait in the living room or outside waiting for them to finish. I figured he wanted to spend some time alone with her. Some days, it would frustrate me but, he was my ride to work so I had no choice but to go with him.

Her niece finally moved in with her aunt and we were introduced. I have to admit, she was very attractive – I was not expecting her to be so beautiful...typical cliché! They left us alone to communicate but it created an awkward moment for us. She smiled at me and I smiled back at her and that was all that we could do partly because she did not speak English and I only knew a few words in Spanish. We did what we could to communicate, but it was very difficult.

We were both feeling uncomfortable. I do not know if it was the environment or the inability to communicate that made it feel uncomfortable. It could have been the fact that we were put in a position that forced us to meet. I asked her if she would like to go outside for a walk, and said ok. There was a nearby park that we walked to. She understood English, but had trouble speaking, and I understood Spanish, but had trouble speaking. I had a few female friends here and there, so I was not uncomfortable talking to women, I just never had a girlfriend before. We talked for a while. She noticed my struggles speaking Spanish and would giggle at my words. Her giggles seemed to calm my nerves.

Somewhere during the night, she leaned over and kissed me. Her kiss was soft and sweet, almost innocent. She made me feel good after all my struggles trying to communicate with her! Her kiss felt different from my previous experience with my friend from Virginia, who was aggressively trying to stick her tongue down my throat. I do not know if her kissing me was her way of telling me that she liked me! Her kissing me set me at ease! In a way, I was intimidated by her. I felt inexperienced. She married young and divorced shortly after. In dealing with her divorce, her mother asked her sister (her aunt) if she would allow her to move in with her while she healed. I had to go to work, so I asked her if I could take out on a date! She smiled and said...: -Yes! We went on several dates and spent countless hours talking on the phone. I started to enjoy going to my uncle's girlfriend's house because I was able to spend time with her. Some days, they had to work late so, we would go in early and take them dinner as they were leaving.

She taught me how to kiss among some other things. I was never intimate with her though the desire grew stronger every day. She made me feel happy! I liked the concept that someone was thinking about me and enjoyed spending time with me! It was starting to feel like I was in a relationship, though I never officially asked her to be my girlfriend. I thought by going out on dates and spending time kissing made her my girlfriend.

One night, my uncle had the night off and decided he wanted to go to a party his girlfriend was throwing. He knew I could not call in sick, so I went to work. My uncle had asked my older brother to accompany him, in case he was too drunk to drive home. My brother had no interest in Latino women: he only had an interest in white American girls.

My brother had been going through a difficult period with his high school girlfriend. At the party, he was introduced to my girlfriend and as my uncle went into the room with his girlfriend. I do not know if my uncle and his girlfriend introduced them to each other or they made it known that she was my girlfriend, but somehow, my brother and my girlfriend started kissing.

After the party my uncle and his girlfriend went into his girlfriend's bedroom to retire for the night. In the morning my uncle found my brother and my girlfriend asleep on the sofa. This put my uncle in a difficult situation because he would get his drugs from me. Because he was my uncle, I was very generous with him giving him twice the amount of product for the normal price. He knew that if he kept that secret from me, I would be angry and not supply his needs anymore. He felt guilty and he let me know what had happened.

Once again, I was met with disappointment — I could not believe that just as life was starting to look up, something would prevent me from being happy. I liked her a lot and I thought that she liked me in return. The more time I spent with her, the more my feelings were starting to grow. Our communication was improving and our kisses were becoming more passionate. She would teach me words in Spanish and I would do the same for her in English. I had brought her home to meet my grandmother and that meant something special to me. I was eighteen years old and I had my first girlfriend. I felt we had a good thing going between us.

There was no point in getting upset with my brother. He was an opportunist. He took advantage of the situation. He had no interest in her. My brother and I got into a physical altercation, a few months before this occasion. I do not know if he slept with her out of anger and wanted to hurt me, or if he was just at the right place at the right time. It turned out, as my girlfriend was healing from her divorce, she was in no rush to embark into another relationship. She just wanted to enjoy her life and the company of someone who can meet her needs. In my innocence, I did not notice that she wanted a physical relationship with no strings attached.

How could I allow myself to be put into a situation, where I knew how the story would end? My life was filled with deception! This should have been no surprise. I was angry, but I did not know with whom I should be angry. Should I have been angry with my uncle for taking my brother to the party? Should I have been angry with my girlfriend knowing he was my brother? Should I have been angry with myself for allowing myself to believe that she was interested in me? Or, should I have been angry that I wasn't intimate with her? I hated life once more! This was the third time everything was ripped away from me.

The following day, I asked my uncle to either drop me off at work while he visits his girlfriend or go straight to work. I did not want to see her. On the days they had to work late would be a problem. For the first couple of days, I would stay outside in the car waiting for her and her aunt to leave. She would ask my uncle if I could call her to talk. A few times, she would stay waiting for me to clock in so she could talk to me. She would talk to me but... I would only ignore her. She knew I was upset with her. She would go home, cook, and bring me dinner. I would give it to my uncle and tell him it was from his girlfriend. Had she been honest with me in the beginning and just told me she was not interested in a relationship, I would have probably not have allowed myself to get emotionally attached to her.

I felt it was time for me to either quit or look for another job. I had come to enjoy working at the factory. The people were great and I was making a decent wage, besides, my best clients were employees. I had turned eighteen a few months before I started working at the factory so I was officially an adult yet, I did not have a driver's license or own a car.

I knew I had to make some changes! I knew that I could not get another job without a driver's license and a car. I was not hurt that my girlfriend had slept with my brother; I was disappointed in myself. I was desperately in love with an idea that I had no clue how to make possible with so much adversity around me! My uncle and I lived with my grandmother. Her husband grew tired of the constant drinking and drugs, and separated from her. My uncle and I split the cost of the bills and we took care of my grandmother (his mother). I did not have to tell my grandmother what had happened, because she always knew – even with her drinking she always knew. She would sit me down in the kitchen table and always remind me: "Do something with your life, man!" Then she would laugh and remind me that it wasn't the alcohol talking. She saw the anger and disappointment in me.

I told my grandmother that I wanted to save up and buy a car. I had plenty of money but I had no idea how to buy a car. The next day, as I prepared for work, she made me a meal before I went in to work. As I ate, she went into her bedroom and came out with a large amount of money she had been saving. While I lived with her, I would give her large amounts of money every week to pay the bills, and have enough for her beer and groceries. From all the money I was giving her, she saved a substantial portion and gifted it to me to purchase my car! I tried to refuse it, but you do not refuse a grandmother...so, we bought my first car together! My first car! A 1969 Chevy "El Camino." She was not the prettiest car to look at, but she was loud, scary and...fast!

Having my car gave me the confidence to feel I was in control of something. I decided I would work for a few more weeks, and then find a new job. It was time for a change. It was no longer about avoiding my ex-girlfriend, but about becoming independent! I had spent so much time with my uncle and at work that I forgot about myself.

I was no stranger to starting over and a new job would have provided a fresh start. I felt the timing was right! After I bought my car, I decided to give the supervisor my two weeks' notice. That night, I was going to inform him of my decision, but a new gentleman started. The supervisor asked me to work with him and train him on the molding machine. I spent a few days training him before they allowed him to work on his own. He was appreciative of the effort I made to train him, so much so that he would bring me tacos that his wife made. He was a nice gentleman, approachable and easy to engage in conversation. I would spend my break time eating and talking with him.

There was no hiding the scent of marijuana saturated on my clothes, but he never avoided me because of it. He treated me with respect despite that I still dressed and talked like a gang member. And once again, I could not understand why he would take the time to talk to me. There was something different about him I could not pinpoint.

An inner voice told me to hold off giving my two-week notice. The graveyard shift consisted of younger and middle-aged men full of issues. He was an older gentleman, very soft-spoken and eager to help anyone. I enjoyed having conversations with him; he was very interesting and had a lot of great stories. One night, his conversation went into overdrive. I asked him why he moved from Iowa. He said that, he was a pastor and was asked to take over the church he had started back in the '80s. He asked me if I ever went to church. I let him know that I had been visiting a church when I was a bit younger. He asked why I stopped going. I explained to him the story and how my friend's family was helping me get closer to God but they had moved. I then got mixed up with some bad people and I stopped going. He asked me if I would ever consider going back to church one day. I simply smiled and said: One day!

Out of curiosity, I asked him, what church was he going to pastor? He told me the name of the church. It was a complete shock. I told him that was the church I was visiting a few years back. I mentioned to him the name of the youth pastor that was directing the Bible studies. It turned out, he was the youth pastor's uncle. I asked him if he knew the family that invited me to church, and he said: "Yes!" They were the family that moved to Iowa to help him with the church.

It all seemed surreal. He was offered to pastor the church he established and felt God was directing him back to Florida. I felt a sense of peace come over me! I was happy to know that things were working out in his favor. I asked if the family came back with him.

He said: "No, they stayed in Iowa." I asked how the family was doing and he dropped his head. He mentioned that after they arrived in Iowa, the kids had drifted away from the church. They got involved with the wrong crowd and made some bad decisions. The parents wanted to stay in Iowa to help the new pastor, and wanted to be close to their kids.

I felt that God was trying to talk to me! God did not want me to give my two weeks' notice because He wanted me to speak with this gentleman. I was a mess. I had turned my back on God, stopped going to church, dealt drugs, and hurt people. What would God want with me? I was confused over all that he had been telling me! I wanted to quit and run out of there, yet something inside kept encouraging me to stay a bit longer.

At the request of my friend's mother years ago, my friend would talk to me about God. His tactic was to scare me through the book of Revelations, the end of the world, and going to Hell if I did not accept Jesus into my heart. I had accepted Jesus into my life out of fear, but I never had an encounter with Him. The youth pastor would teach Bible studies, and I understood what he was teaching me, but no one ever taught me what it was to have an encounter with God. Was I having an encounter with God?

Chapter 5

A Real Encounter with God

Almost a year ago, I was sitting in my grandmother's house with a beer in my hand struggling whether to drink it or not. For over a year, I didn't care about anything or anyone. Then things seemed to be turning around for me. Work was going well! I had a girlfriend and I had money in my pocket. Then, like every chapter in my life, I started to lose everything.

Just as I felt like giving up, God had sent this man into my life! He had never spoken to me or any of the other guys about Jesus or church until then. He mentioned plenty of times that he was a pastor of a church, but he never pressured anyone, he never quoted scriptures, or brought a Bible to work. He never made any attempts to speak to any of the guys at work that was not work related; there was something about him that attracted everyone to want to talk to him.

He was always very respectful and willing to help anyone. The guys at work would ask him for prayers. He would come back later and tell the guys that he presented their prayers at the prayer meetings the church held. Though he never spoke to me or anyone directly, he was God sent. He had something that I wanted but... I did not know what it was or how to get it.

I felt torn between quitting work and running away, and running back to the God and the church that I had accepted a few years ago. How could this be? What would God want with me? I felt unworthy of even thinking of going back to church after all that I had done.

This man never invited me to church. He never asked me to give up the drugs. He was never judgmental of me even after knowing that I had accepted Jesus into my life. Every day I worked with him he would smell the scent of marijuana on me yet, he never avoided me or tried to make an excuse not to talk to me. There was something about him that brought conviction to my life.

In a way, I enjoyed the life I was living. I was getting used to the fact that every time something good happened to me, I would eventually end up losing it. I liked my girlfriend a lot and it was depressing to know that my brother slept with her, but I had a feeling that things with her would not last long. I figured it was too good to be true. I felt I was a good person. I consumed and sold drugs, but I was not an evil person. I helped my family as much as I could, even though some of the money did not come from a good place. Nonetheless, I felt an internal battle inside of me. I felt torn between two paths.

One path would continue to lead me towards the same misery that I had been used to; and the other down a path that may allow me to have the marriage and family that I longed for. Was there still hope that I could have a good life? If so, why after so much adversity was God allowing me a second chance? There were no words to describe my confusion. I tried not to think about the conversation I had with the pastor. The voice inside me that told me not to give my two-week' notice started to grow stronger. I could not turn off the voice. The voice would constantly remind me of the church and my acceptance of Christ. I would remember the Bible study lessons that the youth pastor would give me. I tried to drown out the voice by getting high, but they only got stronger; I could not escape it!

One night, my uncle did not want to drive to work and asked me if I could take him. I said: "Sure." It had been a couple of weeks now that things had blown over with the ex-girlfriend. I told my uncle I would take him, but I would not go to his girlfriend's house. He agreed to the terms.

Since my conversation with the pastor, I had slowed down my consumption of marijuana. I felt a strong conviction to quit. I attempted to quit smoking, but it was a difficult challenge. Not because I was so addicted, but because I really enjoyed getting high. One night, my uncle wanted to get high before we went into work. It didn't seem strange; it was something we did every day. That night felt different! I tried to stop smoking but something always called me back to it. Living with my uncle was not helping me quit. I did not want to smoke because of what I was feeling, but my uncle was persistent and I gave in. After we consumed the drugs, a dark feeling of fear came upon me. I could not explain it, but I felt that something was wrong. We got to work and I tried to work through the fear. I thought it was probably the grade of marijuana was too potent and I was experiencing a deep high.

I tried to brush it off, but the feeling was overwhelming. I started to hear voices in my head. Not like the voice that told me not to hand in my two-week notice. These voices were different, almost suicidal. The fear was so intense! I had to tell the supervisor I was not feeling well. I asked if I could go home sick. I told my uncle I was leaving, and he just said: "Be sure you come to pick me up in the morning."

Of all days to ask me for a ride to work, this happens. I left work but I knew I could not go home. I remembered the pastor telling me he lived close by. He had given me his number a few weeks back, because he transferred from the night shift to the day shift. He said if I ever needed to talk, I was welcomed to call him at any time. I called him, but he was not home. His three sons were there and the middle son answered the phone. He was around my age. I asked for his father, but he informed me that he had left for the weekend to speak at an event. I explained to him that I needed to speak with him and it was important. He asked me if there was anything, he could help me with. In my desperation, I said: - "I need to speak to someone!" He offered to speak to me. He gave me instructions on how to enter the community and gave me the code to enter through the community gates. I was in no condition to drive. I was going crazy! I had the shakes and felt feverish. I had hundreds of thoughts racing through my head and I could not concentrate. The closer I got to their house, the more intense the voices grew. The pastor lived around the corner from work, so I knew that if I could just make it there, I would be ok. I did my best to drive as carefully as I could.

It was close to midnight when I got to their house. I had met the pastor and his wife, but I had never met his kids. The pastor mentioned once that he had three boys around my age. I was unsure of speaking to them about what was going on inside of me. I thought, "What would they know?" I got to the door and they let me in. I could sense their fear in them, but they let me.

Upon entering, I felt a spirit of peace and conviction come upon me, and I was no longer feeling afraid. It had been a couple of hours since that I consumed the drugs. I am sure they were able to smell the marijuana on my clothes. I want to say that the effects of the marijuana faded away as I walked in, but deep inside I knew, there were spiritual forces fighting inside of me. In an instance, the voices in my head stopped. The thoughts of suicide went with it, and I felt free.

His three sons gathered around me (the youngest son told me - months later- that before I came into their home, he had placed a baseball bat nearby just in case). The middle son asked me what was wrong. I felt the urge to let it all out but I didn't know how to start. I paused for moment thinking, and then, I cried out to and explained everything to them. I explained how messed up my life was. I told them how I had just given up on life and succumbed to the life that I inherited from my family. I told him about his father and how he had been a blessing to me. I mentioned to him my acceptance of Jesus, years ago.

The middle son looked at me and said: "The first thing I have to ask you is, are you still willing to give your life to Christ?" I thought I gave it to Him years back. I was confused about my acceptance. It could have been that I was never serious about Jesus the first time. I accepted Jesus because I liked my friend's sister and I did not want to go to hell!

In my confusion, I nodded my head, and said: "Yes." He asked if he could pray over me. No one ever asked to pray over me when I first accepted Jesus. I was asked to raise my hands and repeat a simple prayer: "Lord, I know that I am a sinner in need of your forgiveness. I stand before you, Jesus, this day asking you to come into my heart... I accept you as my Lord and Savior. Amen!" I repeated those words and was sent back to my seat. He prayed over me and asked God to have mercy on me and to forgive me of my sins. His prayer felt real and sincere. I could sense that he had a real relationship and trust in God. After we prayed, we talked for a few more hours. I came in thinking they were just kids, I left knowing they were God sent. They recommended I speak to the senior pastor in the morning about all that had happened.

They gave me his contact information and invited me to visit them at church the following Sunday. I had not realized how late it was and how much time they had spent ministering to me! They were tired and almost falling asleep on me. I had to pick my uncle up from work in just a few more hours so; there was no point in going home.

I was feeling better. I decided to go to a Denny's that was close by, and wait for my uncle. I picked up my uncle and went home. It had been a long night, and I was exhausted but could not fall asleep. I was replaying all that had happened! I knew I had to call the senior pastor, but I felt nervous about calling him.

Would he answer my call? Would he be willing to speak with me? The previous senior pastor of the church was not approachable and only spoke Spanish. I did not know if I would be able to communicate with him. Would he be upset if I called him? I had all of these uncertainties running through my head! I thought about waiting for the associate pastor to come back and speak with him. Then, I started to think what if I had another incident like the one I just went through. I did not want to experience something like that again. I worked up the nerve and called the pastor. I was praying that he would not answer the phone, but... he answered the phone and I froze! I stood silent for a second. He said in this soft voice: "Hello, you have reached senior pastor of the Apostolic church, can I help you?" His voice was so calm and peaceful! It gave me the confidence to respond. I told him my name and I let him know how I received his contact information. He said he was waiting for my call.

Turned out, the associate's pastor's middle child had called him and informed him what had happened, and he should be expecting a call from me. The pastor asked me, if I was available to come to his house to speak with him. He gave me his address, and I went to speak with him at his home. I was tired and had not slept, but I went anyways. I had never spoken to a pastor! As a child, going to church –on the Baptist school bus – was fun, but it did not feel like a church service. They played games; had a lot of short skits and we ate a lot of free food! We never had any contact with the pastor of that church.

The children's ministry had a young married couple that would minister to the kids, but the pastor was never directly present. So many kids attended their service through the school bus ministry, that it seemed more like a fun hangout than a church. I was nervous about what he might say. As I drove to the pastor's house, I was praying that he would be a kind-hearted man like the associate pastor was. His voice on the phone was peaceful, but there's only so much you can tell from a voice. I pulled into his driveway.

I was having second thoughts as to whether I should go in or turn around and go home. As I sat there in the car, his wife opened the front door to let their small dog out. She waved at me and said: "Are you here to speak with my husband?" There was no way of escaping now! I got out of my car and said: "Yes!" She welcomed me in warmly and took me to his office. She was a very nice lady!

The pastor was sitting at his desk when I came in. He got up, came over to me and shook my hand. He introduced himself to me. He was an older gentleman, about the same age as the associate pastor. He welcomed me in and asked me to sit down.

He offered me something to drink and made me feel at ease. He asked: How could he help me? I was so nervous... I did not know what to say or how to begin. He noticed that I was nervous. He then started to ask me simple questions to break the ice. "How old are you? What do I do for work? How long have I lived in the area, etc....?" After a few questions, I started to open up, and felt comfortable enough to speak to him about what had happened.

I explained to him all that had happened! I started to tell him the whole story, since I first met my friend and his family. I told him how dysfunctional my family was, and how I was constantly being hindered in every attempt to be happy.

I explained to him how I had accepted Jesus into my life once, but I came to find out later that I had been scared into accepting Jesus. I was doing all of the talking! I spent a few hours with him going over every detail of my life's story that would be pertinent to our conversation. I saw on movies before that people would go to Catholic churches for confessions and talk about all the things that were bothering them. I felt that was what I needed to do as well.

He sat there listening to all that I had to say! He never questioned anything or interrupted. He never cut me off from anything that I was saying. He was patiently waiting for me to finish. Once I ran out of words, he sat and looked at me. He asked me if he could ask me an important question.

I said sure, thinking he was going to dig into my past or possibly ask me if I was on currently on drugs. Before I went to his house, I made sure to have showered and changed my clothes. I did not want him to smell the marijuana on me. His question was simple: "So, what do you want to do?" I sat there silently for a few minutes thinking about a response. To be honest, I did not know how to respond to that question. I did not know what I wanted to do!

I had an idea of what I have always wanted, but I didn't know how to make it happen. I did not know if it was possible to break those chains that had burdened my family for generations. One thing that I knew was certain, just hours before: I had made a decision to follow through – once again – in accepting Jesus back into my life!

I had no other choices. I wanted to give my life fully to Christ. So, I responded: "I want to get baptized and make it official!" He said: "That is what I wanted to hear." I knew there was nothing he could do for me, if I didn't know what I wanted.

He offered me Bible studies, once again! I explained to him that I had already received the studies and I felt sure about what I wanted! I just wanted to proceed with the baptism. He asked again if I was sure, and I said: "Yes… I'm sure!"

I did not want to waste any more time than I had already wasted. He made the arrangements for me to be baptized the upcoming Sunday. I went to church nervous that Sunday. It had been almost two years since I last set foot in a church. I did not know if some of the same people were going to be at church. As I walked in the church building, I was greeted by the middle son who had ministered to me. The youth pastor was back in church and he approached me and greeted me as well. They made me feel welcomed.

As I approached the baptism tank, I was questioning myself if I was making the right choice, and if I was ready. Moments before the baptism would take place; the pastor calls me before the congregation and asks me a question: "For how long do you plan to serve the Lord?" I didn't know I had an option to choose for how long. I did not know how to respond to that question.

I was regretting not taking the Bible studies again. If I would have taken Bible studies, I would have known how to respond. Not knowing how to respond, I replied: "For as long as I am permitted, I will serve the Lord." The pastor prayed over me and led me to the baptism tank.

I was an official Christian! There was no turning back now. Coming up from the waters, I was expecting some miraculous events take place. I remember my grandmother having a picture of Jesus getting baptized and a scripture that read: "He heard a voice from heaven saying, this is my Son, in whom I am pleased."

There was nothing miraculous coming out of the waters for me! No voice from heaven and no trumpets blasting. At the end of the day, it was just me and a clean conscience. I got out of the water and went to change in the men's room.

The pastor told me they had a surprise for me as soon as I got dressed. I came back into the sanctuary and I was met by all of the members of the church. The pastor gathered everyone and said: "Let us pray for our new brother that his faith fails him not."

The members gathered around me and prayed for me. After they had prayed for me, they had a cake. The youth pastor presented me with my first Bible. I had never owned a Bible in my life. I had made so many mistakes in my life: I had hurt so many people, I stole and had gotten into many physical altercations, I had let my mother down and abandoned my siblings. The first part of my life was filled with so much anger and disappointment. Could it have been possible for God to forgive me for all that I had done? As I left the church, I could only think of how unworthy I felt to have my sins forgiven? How was it even possible? I was scared, but... in a good way!

I had to start over several times in my life, but I could not anticipate what would be next for me? One thing I was certain, I did not want to fail in my faith just as the pastor had prayed over me. I did not know the first thing about what it meant to be a Christian! My grandmother had given her life to Christ years ago, but she had drifted away. I did not want the same to happen to me! I made a promise to God to serve Him, as long as I was permitted to do so and I was determined to do so!

Chapter 6

My Journey into Marriage

My conversion into the Christian faith was sudden. It was years in the making, but I was baptized from one day to the next. Two years had passed since I received Bible studies from the youth pastor and it helped me to understand the meaning of baptism and the reasons one should confess their sins and be washed from them.

But... I was questioning even after the baptismal service, if I had made the right choice.

It had been two years since I stopped going to church. The service was different! The senior pastor had implemented some changes to make the church modern and attractive. The pastor preached in a way that I could understand and to which I could relate. His Spanish was simple. The music was modern. The musicians were the same, but they had worked over the years to bring in new worship songs. It sounded great!

After the celebration, I did not know what I was supposed to do. For a moment, I felt lost. I stayed until everyone had left. The only one left was the pastor and I. He noticed how confused I was! The senior pastor asked me if I would be willing to check the restrooms, to ensure that the trash was taken out, and looked presentable. I didn't mind. I checked the restrooms and made sure they were clean.

After I came back, he asked me if I had any plans and I said: "No." He must have noticed how confused and nervous I was. He asked me if I wanted to join his family for dinner and I said: "Yes." It was all new to me. I followed him to his house. When I arrived, he welcomed me in and introduced me to his children. On my way to his house, the only thoughts that were running through my head was, "Why didn't I go home and shower first?" When I arrived, the associate pastor's middle son was there. I felt comfortable knowing he was there.

I only met him once before, but out of the three brothers, he had helped me the most. The associate pastor's middle son was dating the senior pastor's daughter. He was a great person. He had a noble character and was a bit of a jokester. Before dinner, we sat in the living room and laughed at his jokes. The senior pastor's wife made a delicious meal! She placed all the food in the middle of the table. We all sat down for a formal dinner. She made it clear to everyone; no one was allowed to touch the food until the prayer was said.

We all joined hands and prayed. It felt like a Thanksgiving dinner! It had been over a year that I had a formal dinner with my friend in Virginia, so I was not a stranger to the concept. There was a feeling of peace in their home! The environment felt better than those of the previous families with whom I shared dinner. No one fought, raised their voice, or became upset.

After the prayer, everyone started to fill their plates full of food. I just sat there and observed. The senior pastor's wife was so concerned that my needs were being met, she would constantly tell me to not be ashamed to eat. She would tell me: "Dig in and eat as much as you like, there is plenty more." After dinner, the senior pastor invited me to his office. We sat down and started talking. He asked me about my plans for the future. Up to that point, I didn't think I had a future that I should plan for! My life consisted of a continual: "loving and losing;" the only thing I could plan on is the next time I would lose something I cared about.

I replied that I didn't know. I never knew I had to plan for a future. I thought I would work at the factory or some other factory for the rest of my life. Other than that, I was never in a position that I had to present a plan to someone.

My grandmother was the only person in my life to tell me; "Get up and do something with your life." Why did the pastor care about my plans? I was new in the church. I was certain he had more important people to worry about than my future.

I remembered that my friend's father back in Virginia had asked me once, if I ever thought about going back to school, but he did not question my plans for my future. Looking from the outside; I wondered why my friend's dad, the associate pastor, and now the senior pastor were concerned about me. I came to the church now sober, but still looked and talked like a gang member. The senior pastor had an extensive library collection behind his desk. He stood and turned towards his books. He paused for a moment and pulls out an old book called; "The Pilgrim's Progress." The senior pastor flipped through the pages to check for any notes he may have left in it. He said I could have it on the condition that I would read it. I was not much of a reader. I could not remember the last book I have ever read. I promised I would read it!

"I want you to come every Sunday after church to eat dinner with my family," he said to me. He spent some time talking to me about his life in the ministry and said to me; "I want you to attend Church on Wednesday nights for Bible studies." He said he needed to get me caught up on some Bible studies that would help me better understand how to be a Christian. I told him that I worked the evening shift during the week but I would do my best. It was getting late and I had to work in a few hours. I knew at this point that I needed to look for a daytime job and a few weeks later I found a job at the boat factory.

Before I left, he gave me a serious look and said: "Now I want you to take your faith seriously, do not stop attending service, read your Bible, and I am going to show you how to pray and understand the Bible!"

Why did this man seem to care about me? This was the second time I met him. He was very nice and opened his home to me! His family was different than my best friends and that of my friend from Virginia. Everyone was happy! I am sure they had their issues as every family does, but they all got along so well.

The boyfriend would constantly talk about his marriage with the pastor's daughter. They seemed happy. The pastor's son quickly grew attached to me and later became my best friend. We were inseparable. He was a few years younger than me, but he was as mature as a twenty-year-old. I would go every Sunday for dinner after service. They were having Thanksgiving-style meals every Sunday after church, who does that? They were the real sitcom family of which I had always dreamed.

Working the night shift would be a hindrance to my commitment to the church. We were still working the twelve hour shifts, seven days a week. I felt the timing for a change was right. About a month after my baptism, I spoke with my supervisor and I asked for Wednesday night's off. The company was nearing the finish of the big order and the owner was starting to allow employees two nights off. My uncle wanted to be off Fridays and Saturdays which worked in my favor to have Sunday and Wednesday's off. This would allow me to enjoy the mid-week and Sunday services until I was able to find a new job.

The Bible studies were informative. I was starting to understand why my past was met with many challenges. The scare tactic that my friend had used on me had caused me to live a life fearing God, more than running towards Him. The pastor helped me to understand that there is a loving and merciful side to God.

My friend opened a door for confusion and disappointment towards God. I was traumatized over the fear of dying and going to Hell. For years, I was constantly reminded that the world would be coming to an end, and if I didn't get right with God, I would go to Hell. The pastor was showing me that God works with everyone on a personal level out of love and not fear.

One evening, I felt an urge to ask the senior pastor what it meant to have an encounter with God. It was simple, the conviction that I was feeling when the associate pastor would speak to me, the voice that told me not to put my two weeks' notice, the voice that directed me to the associate's pastor's house, that was God encountering me! He explained to me, God will close every door with the exception of the one door that leads to Him. God wanted to draw me closer to Him so that I would know Him on a personal basis as opposed to a distant figure.

I spent hours learning from the pastor directly. Every Sunday, he would allow me to come into his home for dinner. The family showed me love and acceptance. I could not compare them to a sitcom family. They were better. The brothers and sisters had their arguments, but there was purity to their love. The pastor loved his family and the church. All the church members would come to their house freely dropping off groceries or to spend time with them. They welcomed everyone.

One day, the pastor called me into his office. He had a serious look in his face and asked me to sit down. We had built a great relationship over the past months, and he was more comfortable talking to me. He asked me if I would consider changing my appearance. I would attend church services and go to his house dressed like a gang member. Had he not pointed it out to me, I would have never noticed. It was normal for me to dress with my pants and shirts two sizes bigger.

This was how all my brothers and friends dressed. Since I was the age of fourteen, I would shave the hair off of my head. I loved having no hair on my head. He asked me if I would consider letting my hair grow back as well. The hair would not be a problem but I did not know how I was supposed to dress.

The Pastor had asked the youth pastor if he would spend some time mentoring me. He was always a sharp dressed man. His hair...there is no describing his hair, it almost looked like a plastic mold of hair was on top of his head. It was perfect.

He took me to JC Penney one Saturday and showed me how to pick clothes out. He helped me buy my first dress shirts and slacks. He taught me how to tie the knot on a necktie, and how to combine the necktie with the shirts. Little by little, the pastor was helping me transform into a new person. He would correct my speech so that I would talk more like a respectable young man and less like a street kid. The pastor's wife would indirectly teach me how to treat a lady.

The pastor and his wife grew a love towards me. The pastor's wife later was hired at a factory where my mother was working. I would visit my mom at work to have lunch with her and on occasion, the three of us would spend lunch together. They accepted me into their family! I was just a street kid who sold drugs, and they allowed me not only into their home, but into their family.

The church congregation began to notice how much they had loved me. They began to refer to me as the pastor's adopted son. I loved the pastor, the church, and the congregation. One day, I was doing some work around the church, and one of the members said to me: "Great job, your dad is going to be so proud of you." I had never heard those words! When would I ever imagine that I could make my dad proud? My father was never present for me to try to make him proud of me so how could I know how to make the senior pastor, my new father figure, proud.

I never felt such great love as I did with the pastor and his family! My love towards the pastor grew deeper than a spiritual father, he was my adopted father and his wife was my adopted mother. The feeling was indescribable! This is what I longed for. I was beginning to understand what it was that I was searching for all of these years.

I had always heard people say: "God works in mysterious ways." There are countless ways in which people have had an encounter with God. Some people meet God; at the point of death, others because of an addiction, and some because their lives were in pieces. I was getting to know how great God's love was through the pastor and his family. It would be through this family that ministered to me and showed me how great the love of God could be! I was encountering God through them.

I would spend time with the associate pastor and his three sons as well. They were just as great as the senior pastor and his family. I enjoyed all three brothers. Of the three sons, I had grown attached to the middle son; there was a close connection with him. It was the middle son who had mustered up the courage to minister to me. The youngest was ready with the baseball bat to protect his brothers if the need arose. The family also had accepted a street kid into their home and loved me just as much. There was no more questioning if I had made the right choice of giving my life to Christ.

The following Sunday, the associate pastor and his family were brought before the congregation to be prayed over. The associate pastor came intending to take over the church he founded, but God had other plans for him. A church in Michigan was in need of a pastor and he was offered the church. He had accepted and they would leave the next day. It was a shock to me!

They had helped me so much and now they would be leaving. Upon hearing the news, I wanted to be happy for them, but I had a feeling come over me that I had not felt since I was baptized, the feeling of abandonment. After church, we went out for dinner one last time with them. I went home after dinner and laid down thinking about how much the family had helped me! I was angry with God and asked Him why He would take them away from me. God began to speak to me! He made me aware that they were brought here just for me and just as they had come here to minister to me, He was going to use the pastor and his family to help others like me! I felt a feeling of peace come over me and I was able to be happy for them.

I had been in the church for several months at this point. One day, out of frustration, the pastor said to the congregation, please come to church early so that we could start the service on time. I think I was the only one who received the message. I was the only one who would come in early. Some days, it was just the pastor and me waiting. I would come to church early, and the pastor would find something for me to do; clean the restroom and stock the paper, sweep the entrance, and straighten the pews. I did not mind it.

One Sunday after church, the pastor called me into his office. When I came in, the new associate pastor and youth pastor were in the office. He asked me to sit down. He explained to me that they had been observing me over the past months. I was faithful in tithing and attendance and they noticed my desire to serve in the church. The pastor asked me if I would be interested in joining the ministry. I paused for a moment. I did not know how to respond. My only response was: "What do I have to do?!" He smiled and said: "Nothing! Just keep doing what you have been doing." That seemed easy, I didn't know what I was doing, but it felt good knowing that they had noticed something in me to ask me to be a part of something great.

For the next year, I was put on a probationary period in which I would continue to be observed. I began ministerial classes with the pastor. A year later, the pastors met with me and approved me to go before the bishop and the elders of the district to be interviewed. The interview would determine if I would be initiated as a deacon within the district and within the general assembly. I worked hard to prove that I was a worthy candidate for the ministry.

A year to date, I was presented before the bishop and elders a few months after. There were many candidates in line waiting to be interviewed. We were all nervous! There had been a few candidates come out in tears, because they had been rejected. Others... came out stating that was one of the most difficult interviews they had gone through. I started to get nervous! My name was called and I headed into the interview room. My pastor was one of the elders on the committee. The stress was building inside of me. What were they going to ask me? I entered the room and sat down in front of the panel. The bishop looked at me and asked: "Brother, are you faithful in your tithing?" I responded: "My pastor and elder of the district are witness to my faithfulness." The bishop turned to the elders and asked if they had any questions for me. They nodded their heads no.

The Bishop stood up and congratulated me on becoming an official deacon within the district and the assembly. I would be presented before the district in the convention that was coming up! I shook the Bishop's hand and walked out. I was confused. What happened in there? I sat down and some of the other candidates asked me how it went. All I could respond was, it was good, and I was approved. I sat down thinking they may call me back in for more questions, but they didn't.

The coming convention I was prayed over before the members of the district. For the next two years, I would be placed on another probationary period to determine if I would become an ordained minister. I had a long road ahead of me and needed to continue doing whatever it was that I was doing. To this day, I still cannot figure out what those words meant. The only thing I was doing was showing up to church early, being the last one to leave, cleaning, being faithful in my tithes and attendance, and bringing to church whoever would be willing to come with me.

I was not good at speaking in front of a crowd and unable to sing. The congregation was predominantly Spanish, so communicating was a challenge but I did what I could. I never gave a sermon while I was a deacon. The pastor did allow me to lead worship service but because I could not sing well, it was on rare occasions. He was also allowing me to teach Sunday school to the intermediate youth. By then, my knowledge of the bible was increasing greatly.

Two years had passed and I was approved to go before the bishop and elders once again for an interview for ordination. Over the past two years, I had gained a reputation within the district as being the pastor's adopted son. I was becoming more involved with the different youth from other churches within the district. My pastor was a respected elder within the district and had a great influence with the pastors in the district. My passion to serve not only on the local level but on the district level was becoming noticeable.

I found myself in the waiting room waiting for my name to be called. It was a repetition of my previous experience. Some candidates were accepted and others were rejected. Some candidates had a difficult interview and others came out rejoicing. In this occasion, my attention was shifted to some of the candidates. I failed to notice on the last interview a key component to the interview. Those candidates who were married had had to be interviewed with their spouse present.

One of the candidates stated that his wife was asked some questions in which he was not allowed to answer. If the wife was not in agreement, the couple would be asked to leave the room and discuss their commitment, and wait until next year to be interviewed once again. At the time, I did not understand that concept.

My name was called! I said to myself: "This time I am not going to get so lucky and will be subjected to answer difficult questions." My pastor was still an elder and the bishop had been reelected. The bishop looked at me and said: "Brother, are you still giving your tithes faithfully?" I looked at him and said, "Bishop, my pastor and elder of the district are witness to my faithfulness."

He then turned to the elders and asked if they had any questions for me. They nodded their heads no. The bishop stood and shook my hand and said: "Welcome to the ministry brother. In the upcoming convention, you will be anointed and ordained into the ministry."

I was now a few months into my twenty-first birthday. I would be the youngest ordained minister in our district. I had always admired my pastor for being one of the youngest ordained ministers within our assembly who was asked to pastor a church at the age of sixteen. I wanted to make him proud! I had a strong impression that the pastor did not want his sons in the ministry. The congregation loved him dearly, but it was a struggle. On occasions, I would accompany him as he supervised churches in the district. He would tell me stories of his struggles early in his ministry. I wondered if that was the reason he did not encourage his sons to enter into the ministry.

On our travel to visit churches, he would take advantage of the time to mentor me in the ministry. He saw something in me early on that prompted him to bring me up in the ministry. I knew that becoming ordained would now require more of me. Being a deacon was not easy! I knew being a minister would be just as challenging. I accepted the calling and I felt proud! I did not want to let my pastor down.

I was anointed and ordained a few months later at the district convention. Shortly after the convention, I started to notice small changes in my pastor. Four years had now passed since I came into his home to speak with him. I had grown so attached to him and his family that I failed to set boundaries between church, family, and the ministry.

The senior pastor began demanding more commitment from my ministry. He would get upset if I missed a service or if had to leave early. At first, I thought this was the demands of the ministry. I remembered on one of our travels, he would mention to me how tough his pastor was on him early on in his ministry. I figured this was part of the training. I had been asked to work within the district level, but the pastor demanded I resign because it would interfere with my dedication to the local church.

The new associate pastor, who had become my best friend, once said to me that he felt sorry for me. He encouraged me to stand up to the senior pastor's behavior, but I couldn't. I loved him too much to do such a thing. I was bent on making him proud of me; I did not want to disappoint him. I tried to be as submissive as I could.

The past four or five years were wonderful! My life was falling apart before I gave my life to God. I had been blessed with a great job at a boat manufacturing company; I was offered a manager's position and it came with a large pay increase.

I was rebuilding my relationship with my family, and building my self-confidence. I had enrolled in Bible College and I was leading the youth ministry. God was starting to use me to minister to the lost and I would continue to bring to church whoever was willing. Things were difficult with the pastor, but the blessings far exceeded the abuse, so I thought.

The pastor had called me into his office after a Sunday service. The pastor would have regular meetings after church with the ministers to evaluate the church's progress. It seemed normal for him to call me into his office. The pastor asked me to sit down. I was nearing twenty-two years old.

The associate and youth pastor were present. The pastor looked at me and said: "Brother, I think it's time for you to consider getting married." I looked over to the associate pastor and laughed. I thought he was joking! The pastor said in a serious tone: "Brother, I need you to start considering marriage, because I would not be able to use you much further in the ministry."

I could not believe what he was telling me. I looked at the associate and youth pastor thinking to myself... is this a serious conversation? I replied to the pastor: "Pastor, first of all, there are no single women in the church; and second, I am not ready for marriage."

There were other factors involved in my decision, but I did not feel ready for marriage. I wanted to further my ministry. I wanted to spend some time in the missionary field, and I wanted to visit other churches within the assembly. I wanted to enjoy and develop my ministry!

As the weeks passed, the pressure started to intensify. Every Sunday consisted of the same questions: "Have you considered marriage? Are you making yourself known to the single ladies in the district?" The pastor would bring me before the congregation to pray over me, so that the Lord would bless me with a wife. It was overwhelming!

No matter how much I pleaded that I was not ready for marriage, the more he would insist and threaten to take my ministerial credentials away. After several times of being called to the front of the congregation to be prayed over for a wife, some of the members would start pressuring me about marriage. I was still learning how to become a man. I was young in the ministry. I not only was a young minister, I was promoted at work and I wanted to focus on my career as well. I was not ready and I wanted to wait. I had some female friends from churches within the district, but I never pursued any of them further than friends. I did not feel it was the right time. Our youth group had grown and we had some beautiful girls but I had other interests at the time.

His daughter had broken up with the previous associate pastor's son. She was a beautiful young lady, but I knew deep inside she did not want any part of the ministerial life. The ministry had been difficult for her and the family. I do not know if this was the reason she ended her relationship, but something inside gave me the impression that she was not interested in the ministry or me.

The pastor's wife had encouraged her to give me a chance. She would also encourage me to talk to her. She would give me insights of things that she liked hoping that I could find common ground with her. We attempted to date but mainly out of pressure from her mom. We went on a few dates, but I knew she was only doing it to please her mother. She felt uncomfortable and I did not want to pressure her even further.

I knew deep inside she would be a wonderful pastor's wife. She was smart, and very mature for her age, and very beautiful. She would have been supportive and encouraging of my ministry given the chance, but it was not a life she would have chosen for herself.

I felt the pastor was not in agreement that I date his daughter. I wanted to ask him if he was ok with me dating her, but I did not get the nerve. Had he wanted me to date his daughter, he would have made the arrangements, but he never asked me if I would consider his daughter, (however awkward that may have been). He knew that his wife was the one encouraging the relationship. In the end, if he did not want his sons to be ministers, why would he want his daughter to marry a minister? I decided to back away.

I am glad that she did not open up to me. I am confident that I would have worked hard to give her a good life; despite how demanding the ministry and church could be. The congregation can have no mercy on its ministers. She eventually met a young man from California and married him. I was happy for her.

The pressure continued for two years! It was taking its toll on me. I had to either get married or give him my ministerial credentials. The pressure was not only from the pastor, but from the congregation as well. I was reaching my boiling point and ready to hand him my credentials.

A young lady had moved to the area and would begin to congregate in the church. She was a nice girl and displayed a love for the church. She was eager to help in the youth ministry and was part of the worship team. She was friendly and easy to talk to. She was a great person after getting to know her but I was not seeking a relationship.

She was a few years younger than me but way more mature. We would hang out with the youth group every weekend. The more time I spent around her, the more I became comfortable talking to her. She became my friend! No matter how intense the pressure was, I could not see her more than just a friend. I did not know if she was interested in me other than a friend but we never spoke about our intentions.

After a few months of congregating, she too was feeling the pressure to give me a chance. We would spend hours talking on the phone, but it was just as friends. The pastor and the congregation would see that we would talk continuously, but they would not let off the pressure. The frustration would be so overwhelming that I did not want to attend church service only to avoid hearing those taunting.

One evening, I was driving her and some of the youth home from an event. We were talking about how cruel the congregation and the pastor were towards us. She opened up and stated said that if she knew the congregation and pastor were going to do this to her, she would not have moved here. I apologized to her and I tried to let her know that I had no part in it. She understood. She knew that I was not looking to get married so soon. I had expressed to her that I was not ready.

My senior pastor had been her pastor when she was younger. Her family loved him! This was one of the reasons why her family decided to move here and congregate with us. She could not believe he was encouraging this behavior. She, too, was feeling overwhelmed. As a side note, I had a slight interest in someone else within the district and had attempted to get to know her. I tried to be discreet about it so that no one would pressure her, but the pressure locally was too intense to pursue a long-distant relationship, (this was before smartphones and social media were available).

The pastor and congregation were fixated on seeing us date. One day, I asked her if she would consider the possibility of us getting to know each other more than friends. She was honest and said to me: "Had there not been all the pressure, it may have been easier to answer you." I told her I understood. She asked me if I had an interest in her. I replied to her: "I really enjoy talking to her and she was a great person, but I, too, was feeling the pressure." She asked me what I wanted to do. I figured at this point, there were no other options for me. I said to her that if she was willing to give this a chance, I would be open to seeing how things worked out.

She accepted to view our relationship from a more intimate perspective than just as friends. She knew that I was an ordained minister and was aware of the pressure that the senior pastor put on me to continue in the ministry. I explained to her how much I loved the ministry. I made it clear, if God was going to call me to become a pastor, an evangelist, or a missionary that that would be the life I wanted to pursue. If she did not want any part of that life, it would be fine for us to remain as friends, and never bring up the subject of us going any further.

She responded: "My father has been in the ministry for over twenty years. My mother who passed away was a minister's wife. I know what the lifestyle consists of, and I know the lonely nights my mother faced. I know the countless questions from my brother and me asking when was dad coming home. I know about the financial struggles, and I know how harsh the congregation can be. You are a great minister and I would love to be a part of your ministry! I will support you and help you."

Of all the things she said to me, what stood out the most was her response: "I would love to be a part of your ministry and I will support you." Those were the only words I needed to hear from her. We had built a strong platonic friendship over the past two years as friends.

I liked her as a friend, but I was not romantically attracted to her. I did not have strong feelings for her that would transition into a marital commitment, but I felt that if this was the person that God was bringing into my life, He would ensure that our love would grow.

With all the pressure I was feeling, I was not thinking as I should have. I should have stood firm on my decision to wait but I did not want to lose my ministry and I did not want to disappoint my pastor. I don't know if I based my decision out of love for the ministry, my love for the pastor, or because I was in love with the idea of marriage and – eventually having my own sitcom family. One thing I knew for certain, I wanted the pressure to stop!

We made it official but even then, the pressure was still present. I gave in after two weeks and asked her if she would marry me. She said: "No!" She wanted me to propose to her the right way and with a ring. She wanted to have a special moment when asked to marry. So I saved up some money and bought her a ring. I took her to a nice place and I knelt and proposed to her… and she accepted! We agreed to get married a year later.

Chapter 7

The Signs

I heard a short story once about a man whose boat capsized deep in the ocean and was on the verge of drowning. He pleaded with God to save him. A man with a small fishing boat pulled next to him wanting to throw him a life jacket. The man in the water said: "No, thank you, God is going to save me!"

A large ship came by and lowered a ladder to him, and the man said once again: "No, thank you, God is going to save me!" Then… a helicopter came by and dropped him a rope, once again he replied: "No, thank you, God is going to save me!" The man drowned and went to heaven before God showing disappointment with Him. The man was questioned as to why he was disappointed with God. The man replied: "I called out for you to save me and you allowed me to drown."

God explained to the man that He tried to save him on three occasions but he rejected God's help each time." The man asked God, "How did you try to save me three times?" God revealed to him that he was sent a small fishing boat to throw him a life jacket and pull him in, then he was sent a large ship that let down a ladder so that he could climb up, and last he was sent a helicopter to lower a rope to pull him up. God was trying to save him! He was too naïve to see the signs that the help was coming from God."

It is easy for us as humans to get into trouble and become disappointed with God for allowing all the wrong that happens in our lives. It is easy to be naïve to His voice or the methods He uses to direct our decisions. Our own foolishness can deceive us. God is always present! We get disappointed because we expect God to work according to our way of thinking. He hears us and He responds, maybe not in the way that we want Him to, but He responds.

There comes a time; after ignoring all the warning signs that He decides to step back and allow us to drown. Not because He is cruel, but because we take it upon ourselves to make decisions that are not according to His purpose and will. I failed to notice all the warning signs that were present. I was asked once what I thought would be the ideal age to get married and have kids. It was an interesting question. I envisioned twenty-four as good age to get married and twenty-six to have children. In doing the math, if I had a child at twenty-six, when the child was ten years old, I would be at a young age and able to be active with the child.

When the child turned twenty, I would be forty-six. The child would now be an adult and independent. That would allow my wife and me to be at an age that would allow us to travel and see the

118

world. The idea seemed feasible! I thought I would model my marriage in this fashion. It was a safe plan! What could go wrong?

I called the pastor and informed him that I had made a decision to enter into a relationship and was considering marriage. I thought he was going to be happy and give me some words of encouragement. His response was very dry and cold. He asked me if I had set a date.

I told him a year to date. He said if I needed anything to let him know. I was expecting him to act not only as my pastor, but more as the father figure to the spiritual son I had become and he had come to love. Something did not feel right...this was what he had been pressuring me about for the past two years.

The Sunday that followed, the pastor called a meeting with ministers and leaders. Our meetings were always after the Sunday service. He notified everyone that the meeting would be before Sunday school and we needed to come early. The pastor made the announcement that he had put in a request to be transferred to either Arizona or New Mexico. A church opened in that area and he would be leaving within a couple of months as soon as the assembly could find a replacement.

It was not a surprise. The senior pastor's wife was from New Mexico and their eldest daughter had married and moved to Arizona. The church had known for years that he desired to move West to be closer to their family, but God had not allowed the change. He almost came close to moving before my encounter with God.

The senior pastor received notice that a senior pastor in Arizona was considering retirement; the senior pastor from FL was asked to replace the pastor once the Arizona pastor's retirement took effect. The assembly reached out to the associate pastor who moved to Iowa to come to FL. It turned out that the senior pastor in Arizona delayed his retirement causing the senior pastor to remain in Florida until such position was vacant in the future; and the associate pastor, having no place in the FL district, was asked to take over a church in Michigan. God had other plans for them both! It made me feel so small knowing that God had a plan for me that was bigger than what I could have imagined.

The senior pastor's daughter had met a young man from California. They had been corresponding through the internet for some time, and they decided to get married. She had always dreamed about moving to California and finally had her opportunity. She married and moved without hesitation. Her brother decided he wanted to join her and asked if he could move with her. This had given the senior pastor enough motivation to want to move.

God had finally opened the door they had all been waiting for! He would announce to the congregation in the Sunday service about his decision. I could not believe this was happening. I had been down this path several times before. The pastor saw my disappointment and asked me to join him for dinner after the service to talk.

The pastor knew my entire history and I would always open up to him when I needed his advice. I was his adopted son! He was aware that my greatest struggle in life was overcoming the feeling of abandonment. I needed his comfort at that moment. We went to dinner and talked for several hours.

I asked him if he would allow me to move with them. He assured me that I was strong enough to overcome my struggles and besides, he wanted me to stay and help the church during the transition. He knew the church would struggle and they would need a familiar face to be neutral during the transition.

I was confused. I had been struggling for the past several years, trying to convince him that I was not ready for marriage and he would continually pressure me. He threatened to remove me from the ministry if I did not marry and, now, I had committed myself to marry someone and he was moving. This did not make sense!

The congregation had been made aware of my engagement, and that I would be getting married within a year. I was in too deep to call everything off. The pastor would be leaving in a couple of months, so we decided to push the wedding closer so that he could marry us before he left. I figured that was the least we could ask of him.

I was too young and naïve to stand up for what I wanted. I did not want to disappoint anyone. On one hand; I wanted to be a great husband to my fiancée and great minister to the congregation, but on the other hand, I did not feel God's timing was right. In the end, I succumbed to the pressure and the fear of what people would think if I backed away from the engagement. I never spoke to my fiancée about postponing the engagement now that the pastor was leaving so that we could date freely and take things slower.

Our church was very traditional. Wedding rings were not permitted. She had been raised in the same traditional church since she was born. Her father had deep roots of a traditional minister. She was well aware that ministers and their wives did not wear wedding rings; however, she asked me for an engagement ring. I did not question her motives for wanting an engagement ring. It was strange, but I never questioned her.

She had moved here with her brother. They had purchased a home together a few months after they moved to town. It was a small home that fit their needs. They were both single and were planning on staying permanently in the area. They were older than our other youth but were actively involved with the youth. It was the perfect hang-out for the youth.

One weekend, she had invited the youth to their house for Bible study. The girls had planned on turning the Bible study into a sleep-over. Sometime during the event, she had taken her ring off and placed it on a counter.

The ring had come up missing. She had an idea which of the youth had taken it, but she could not prove it. She informed me of the incident the next day at church. I didn't get upset, but I couldn't help but ask myself how could she have lost it or allowed such an important symbol to be stolen? The first ring was an expensive ring so I did not want to spend more money buying her another ring similar to the one that was stolen. I bought her another ring just as nice but less expensive. We had to save money for the wedding.

I was being blessed at work. I had received another promotion and I was financially stable. I had received offers from some of the congregation to help me with the wedding but I had never been used to receiving help. Work was offering plenty of overtime so I decided I would pay for the bulk of the cost on my own. I planned on paying for everything except the wedding cake and limousine for which her friends offered to pay.

I wanted a small wedding, the congregation with no kids, a few family members, and a few friends. I thought this should be easy! Our church had a small building and would not accommodate a large crowd. We knew we had to rent a church. I found a church nearby that allowed us to use their building for the wedding. I paid the rental fee for the building and had the invitation cards printed out with all the information.

A few weeks after the invitations were mailed out, the church secretary called me. They had made a mistake on their calendar and they could not rent us the building on that day. I would have to change the date or seek out another church. Either way, I would have to pay for new invitation cards with the new information. I eventually found another church for the same date.

The district was holding a yearly youth event. We had made plans on attending. It was normal for us to take separate cars to youth events so that we could bring some of the youth who were not able to drive to the events. There was not a youth in need of transportation that day.

The two of us decided to go together, but she wanted us to take her car. It was a newer model sports car. I didn't mind, my car was not as attractive. It was an evening service, and the sun had gone down as we approached the church. As I turned into the main street leading to the church, I failed to see a speed bump. Being a sports car, it was low to the ground so going over the speed bump felt like I ran over a tree.

The bump caused the oil pan to crack and it began to leak oil. I had to replace it right away. Soon after, the car started to have problems. She began to blame the car's issues with the accident. Since it was my fault, I started to pay for repairs. Eventually, she felt the car was not worth fixing.

We were getting married soon! After the wedding, we would be living together so I thought it wouldn't be a bad decision to buy her a new car. Work was going well and I felt I could afford a new car. I bought her a brand-new car. It was a Kia Sportage. There was nothing Sportage about that car.

I wanted to buy a Toyota Corolla, but the salesman pressured me into buying the Kia. It was twice the car for half the price of the Corolla. Kia had been out for some time, but they were relatively new to the market. I gave in to the pressure. Within weeks of purchasing the car, it began to give us problems. The transmission had to be replaced twice.

The air condition compressor gave out, the throttle-body would get stuck, and the brakes wore out months before the wedding. All signs were pointing: "Do not pass go" but I could not pick up on the signs. I was in way over my head. I had asked my younger brother to be my best man. He was living with me at the time and I really wanted him to be part of my wedding. A few months before the wedding, he had gotten into some legal troubles and was sent to prison. I was faced with another last minute change. The pastor's son who was my best friend moved to California and had no plans on returning.

I was mentoring a young man that came into the church a few years earlier. Next, to the pastor's son, he was a good friend. I asked him if he would be my best man after my brother's incarceration and he agreed. That seemed too easy. On Christmas break, he went to visit his father who lived in Texas. During his visit, he was involved in a serious car accident. He could not walk because of his injuries and had to move to Texas during his recovery. It seemed surreal!

My friend and his family moved back from Iowa. We had lost contact with each other since they decided not to return to church. He met and married someone shortly after he moved down and asked me to be his best man at his wedding. I reached out to him and asked him if he would be willing to return the favor. He agreed on the condition that he not be in pictures with women or next to a woman (i.e., the maid of honor or bridesmaids) because his wife was extremely jealous.

I had an idea of how I wanted the wedding to turn out, but putting it together was met with many dead ends. We had agreed that we would organize the event together, but it turned out that I was handling everything. I was determined to make the wedding happen regardless of the obstacles that I encountered.

I imagined that as an engaged couple, we would share the burden and stress of organizing everything. She would give her input on small things: like the design of the cake, wedding invitations, and the reception venue, but she would not make additional decisions. That should have been the moment that I needed to question my motives, or ask myself: "Who wants to get married?"

I knew there may be some challenges in organizing a wedding, but this was beyond what I could have ever expected. The ring, the church, the situation with my best man, and dealing with the lemon of a car I had just bought my fiancée were taking its toll on me. At one point, I wanted to call off the wedding.

The pastor would be moving soon. I felt stuck! The congregation; our families, and friends were all expecting the wedding. As we moved closer to the wedding date, I began to question myself if I was making the right choice. I did not allow myself to question if she was the right person to marry. It could have been that I was afraid of accepting the answer to that question that held me back from asking myself is she was indeed intended for me.

I had created a mess and I was dragging her into it. Deep down, she was a wonderful person and had always been a good friend. I did not want to hurt her, yet, I never questioned her about her thoughts and feelings about the wedding. I would encourage myself by thinking: "If we can make it past all the chaos, we will be ok".

There were many conflicting issues that kept arising all concerning the wedding. The pressure of marriage came from the senior pastor, yet, not once did he ask me if I had made the right decision or counsel me about my decisions around the marriage choice. The only advice he had ever given me was: "When you decide on marrying someone, make sure to stay within the ministry."

He wanted me to marry either a pastor's or evangelist's daughter. He would be leaving in a few months; I did not have the courage to postpone or call off the wedding. Had I done that maybe the pressure of getting married would have left with him.

The difficulties continued even on the day of the wedding. She had asked for a puppy as a Christmas gift a few months before the wedding. Like all dogs, he was chewing everything he could get a hold of. On the day of the wedding, I picked up her wedding dress from the cleaners and took it to her. She laid it out on the bed while in the shower. The puppy came into the room and chewed off the lacing and string of beads on the dress. She became hysterical! Her maid of honor was able to make the dress look presentable but the alteration was noticeable.

The secretary from the second church that we rented for the ceremony called me two days before the wedding. One of their members had passed away and they needed to use the building after our ceremony. They asked me to be prompt with the hours so they could hold their service. They would have a funeral after the wedding? Who would have figured?

In addition, the driver of the limousine and the photographer had gotten lost. After they arrived, we had to rush the ceremony process. The rental to the limousine was for four hours. The time included the driver's inability to find the directions. After the short ceremony, the driver only had enough time to drop us off at the reception hall. The complications continued to come!

She had a friend who worked at a golf country club. He was able to rent the clubhouse where we could hold the reception. The clubhouse had the community pool behind the building. They offered to close the pool for an extra fee. We paid the fee! We were expecting to have a private venue.

The clubhouse manager failed to send out a notice to the residents that the pool would not be available during the time of the reception. The pool was full of people! It made it impossible to take pictures in the courtyard. I struggled to hide my frustrations and I tried to enjoy the day. It was close to impossible! She would constantly tell me not to worry, it will soon be over! She did not understand that my frustrations stemmed the day that the pastor called me into his office and pressured me to marry. It was not about her or the issues with the wedding. There were forces beyond our control.

The reception ended. I was finally a married man! I do not remember if I was happy it was all over or glad to have the pressure of marriage off of me. I was exhausted. It had been a long day! After the wedding, we had planned our honeymoon to be in Orlando. We decided not to travel after the long day and just stay home and relax. I did not mind losing one day of the hotel reservation. I just wanted to take a shower and lay in bed. Even if we would have driven to Orlando, I knew I was not going to be able to enjoy the night as a normal couple on their honeymoon. Of all days, her menstrual cycle had to start that day.

We made arrangements with work to take a week of vacation. The wedding was Saturday but we were not able to leave for Orlando until Tuesday. She had been going through a heavy menstrual cycle causing her severe cramping and bloating. She was not able to walk. I called the hotel and was able to make arrangements to cancel two days. I was hoping that things would have calmed down after the wedding but they continued. After four days, we made our way to go to Orlando. I had visited a few theme parks with the youth, but neither of us had ever vacationed there. I have to admit, we had a great time!

I had been working diligently to pay for all the costs of the wedding! She had been unemployed for a few weeks before the wedding so I carried the burden of the wedding expenses. I worked as much overtime as I could and also found a part-time job at a restaurant to help pay for the wedding and the honeymoon. I desperately needed a vacation.

We finally made it! It took a lot to get here, but we were finally here. All that was left was to enjoy the honeymoon and start living the married life. I thought, "What could go wrong if we had God on our side to help us?"

I had been exposed to what I thought was an ideal marriage and family throughout my life. Some of the families had noticeable flaws, while others seemed perfect. I was finally a married man! This is what I had desired since I was a child watching sitcoms. I was beyond the deep end! Little did I know, I was drowning and God had sent me more than just a life jacket and a ladder.

Chapter 8

Failure upon Arrival

I have heard many people state that the first years of marriage are the best! Around the third year is when you will start to notice problems, and if you can make it past your fifth year, then you know your marriage can withstand anything. This was an interesting concept!

If you are faith-based, you will hear the Bible verse often quoted, "So then, they are no longer two but one flesh. "Therefore what God has joined together, let not man separate," (Mt. 19:6 NKJV)." I have met many people who stand firm on that scripture and believe that their marriage can overcome all difficulties. I have also met others that stand on a different side asking, "If God joined us together, why did He allow us to go through a divorce?

From the day that I met the associate and the senior pastor, I had envisioned myself married; having my own home, a few kids, and having my family just as theirs. It could not get more perfect than that! I wanted to be an example for the rest of my family.

The senior pastor moved two weeks after the wedding.

With all the pressure and torment that he put me through in the ministry, I loved him dearly! He had no reason to take me, a street kid, into his home and love me the way that he and his wife did. Though I was sad, I was forever grateful to have had them in my life. Had it not been for them, I would not have stayed in the church as long as I had.

[When I was twelve I was invited to attend my friend's church and I accepted to fool his mother into thinking I was a good influence on her son. That was my first encounter with the church. This was the plan for us to continue to be friends and also because I was infatuated with his sister.]

The senior pastor taught me how to have a true relationship with God and pure devotion to God; I was young in the ministry and I had a lot to learn. My ministry was growing despite all that I had to endure with the senior pastor over the past 6 years. My job in management was turning into a prosperous career. I worked hard over the years to move up in the company. I was promoted from hourly to salary pay. Everything was falling into place.

Before the pastor moved, we were informed of the new senior pastor coming to lead the church. I had been in the church for six years but I had never heard of this pastor. Those that knew him would state that he was a phenomenal speaker. The new senior pastor had moved in within weeks of the previous senior pastor's departure. It did not take the new senior pastor long to settle in.

Before the new pastor came on board, the associate pastor from El Salvador had informed the ministers that he would not continue to congregate with us after about four years in the church. It was a surprise! The congregation loved him just as much as they loved the previous senior pastor!

The associate pastor from El Salvador fled the country to Mexico during the revolution in the '80s. He pastored and helped establish many churches in Mexico before he migrated to the United States. When the pastor from El Salvador heard who would be leading the church, he resigned from his position without hesitation. He did not give much information other than he knew the pastor personally and of his reputation, so much so, that he resigned leaving with his wife and three children.

The new senior pastor finally arrived after months of anticipation. Being a new minister and at the words of my pastor that "I had to stay and help the church" I called the new pastor and invited him to lunch. He accepted and thought it would be a great way to get to know the ministers.

He asked me at which restaurant I wanted to meet him, but I insisted he choose. He said he was driving around town getting to know his way around and a restaurant had caught his attention. He mentioned to me that he prayed to God and asked that God allow him to eat there. I called him shortly after and his prayer was answered. He told me the name of the place and I met him there at around ten in the morning.

We had a nice breakfast and talked. A few hours into our conversation, the waitress came over and asked if we would be leaving sometime soon. I replied that we had not considered finishing up yet. She said she would be leaving soon because the restaurant would be closing. I asked her: "Isn't this a 24-hour restaurant?" She replied: "Yes! But the restaurant would be closing indefinitely." The owner was forced to close because of a health violation. Seeing her tears, I gave her a nice tip and blessed her.

The first thought that came to my mind was: "This is not a good sign."

During the first month of his arrival, the congregation welcomed him with open arms. The church had been prospering over the past few years. The previous pastor had accepted the church with fifteen members. He worked hard to build the congregation up to one hundred and twenty members. The church's finances were stable and the church was well established. The new pastor only needed to maintain the church's growth.

The first month felt like a revival. His son brought a new sound to the praise and worship gatherings. The pastor spoke in a manner that made you feel as if you were at a convention every Sunday. The congregation felt that he would lead the church to a higher level because he was so charismatic. The previous senior pastor had a very traditional and old fashion style of ministering.

The new pastor was very impressive! He came in with a lot of great ideas and encouraged the congregation to grow further. He indeed was a phenomenal speaker and knew how to motivate the congregation. Within the first month, the congregation became infatuated with him but that didn't last long because he began to show his true nature.

After a couple of months, he became very demanding with the leaders, and exceeded even more from the ministers. He was the total opposite of the associate pastor who moved to Michigan and the senior pastor who had recently moved Arizona. To my surprise, he was the brother-in-law of the youth pastor and the church treasurer.

His son was seventeen and was placed as the music director. His wife became the church secretary, and the sister-in-law remained treasurer. He made it clear right away that no decisions could be made without his approval. It was nepotism at its best. He caused friction within the ministry, and the congregation also began to feel the changes. One by one, the members began to leave the church.

The church was feeling the loss of the associate pastor from El Salvador and his family and now, the youth pastor who was also the brother-in-law decided he would take a temporary leave. He was an important part of the ministry not only for the youth, but also for Sunday school.

He was never one to refrain from speaking when he saw that something was not right. He continually got into disagreements with the pastor. One day, I walked into a conversation they were having in which the pastor told him: "You think because I'm your brother-in-law I would not take your ministry away." I do not know if the pastor noticed me in the room, and he wanted to show his authority, or if he said it to be harsh, but either way, it was enough for the youth pastor to take a leave from the ministry.

The new pastor became indifferent with me and stripped me of every position I held in the church. For the first few months, I tried to stay positive and be neutral for the congregation's sake. The previous pastor must have known something that he did not want to tell me when he asked me to stay and remain neutral.

One day, a young man around my age was invited to the church. I had known his wife from within the district, but I never met him before. He was considering congregating with us. The young man had a successful business and was financially well off. The pastor did everything in his power to coerce him to congregate with us thinking he would bring financial benefits to the church. He was presented to the congregation as a deacon, but we did not know much about him.

Over the years, I have been involved in the district and I was well known. He was never involved within the district level, so I had the impression that he was just a local deacon. Deacons do not have the same functions as ministers within our assembly. They are not considered a lower class of ministers and are respected, but they are ministers in training and are limited in their functions.

The constitution of our assembly has strict guidelines for becoming an ordained minister. Each candidate must pass through a minimum of a two years period as a deacon before getting approved.

It did not bother me that the pastor had stripped me of the positions I held in the church. I had been working diligently over the years in the church, and I could have used the break. As a minister, we have the privilege to sit on the platform behind the pulpit. Ministers are considered overseers and watch over the congregation.

I felt proud that I was a minister and worked hard at it! One Sunday, the pastor asked me to take a seat down with the congregation. He told me he needed the seat for the deacon that would start to congregate. The seating arrangements did not bother me as much as him going against what had been established for decades. I understood he was the pastor and had authority, but why was he going against what was established by the general assembly?

The pressure from him began little by little! I do not know if he felt threatened by me or if he did not trust me. My testimony as a faithful servant to the church, and my love for God was beyond notice. I served the previous pastor and all the associate pastors very attentively. I had offered the same service and loyalty to him as well. The previous senior pastor tested my commitment to the ministry but there was love in the way he treated me because he did not want me to fail as a minister. This pastor, on the other hand, had other motives that were not based out of a love for God and the church.

This pastor began to criticize everything I did. According to him, I did not dress like a minister; he asked me to go out and buy suits that were more to his taste. He stated that my Spanish needed improvement and would not allow me to speak in his church if my Spanish could not be understood. He would question me on my

137

tithes and offerings by calling me into the office and asking me about my salary. He wanted to ensure that I was being faithful in my tithing, something that I had not been questioned about before.

My wife and her brother moved here because of their relationship with the treasurer and her husband. The husband was part of the music ministry. My wife's brother played the guitar and the church was in desperate need of a guitarist. They convinced my wife and her brother to move here and in the meantime, they allowed them to move into their home until they bought their house. They were great friends.

The new pastor called my wife and me into his office one day. His wife and the church treasure (my wife's friend) were present. The pastor begins to criticize my wife, in front of me. The pastor gave her strict orders not to be involved with the youth, as she was a married woman. According to him, her attire did not represent the ministry. I stood silent as a sheep being taken to the slaughter. I did nothing to protect her.

He made it clear to me that my wife was married to a minister and she needed to be present in all activities. After losing her job because of her manager, she started working as a dialysis technician and the job required her to work some nights and two weekends of the month.

We were a young couple. I enjoyed being a part of the men's group as it allowed me to gain their respect as a young minister. My wife did not feel comfortable with the women. They were older than her and she felt she did not fit in. We were in our early twenties and the adults were in their mid-thirties and most all of them had children. She did not fit in.

For weeks to follow, the pastor would call me into his office to speak to me directly. He would, "In light terms," tell me that I needed to be a man and put my house in order. He began to threaten my ministry by telling me that if I did not speak to my wife of her attire, her hair, her makeup, and God forbid, the ring she wore, he was going to have me removed from the ministry.

His wife would call my wife and invite her shopping. My wife had an idea that she was trying to get her to dress like an older woman. My wife did her best to ignore her invites. The treasurer also began to pressure my wife about her attire, her looks, and her commitment to the ministry. She would nicely tell her: "The pastor cares about the two of you, and he wants both of you to be successful in the ministry. He is hard on you because he loves you. "

In my love for the ministry, I would often speak harshly to my wife. She would stay silent and cry as I would tell her what the demands of the pastor were. I would begin to push my frustrations on her. I would remind her that she was a minister's wife and she needed to be obedient to the pastor, no matter how severe he was.

I did not have the slightest clue how the pastor wanted me to dress. I modeled my attire off a traditional Pentecostal preacher. The youth pastor who had taught me how to dress always dressed nicely to service, but he too, was traditional and conservative.

I would go out and buy my wife clothing that I felt were more inclined to a minister's wife. I was indirectly pressuring her. My wife told me plenty of times: "I'm young; I want to dress my age, not like an old lady." The words from the pastor were stronger than her words. I continued to get pressured from the pastor and my wife continued to receive pressure from me.

I was naïve to understand how the pressure was affecting my marriage. We had only been married for a couple of months!

This pastor was not only interfering with my marriage, but he was also draining our finances. It was not just my finances being affected; the congregation was also feeling the financial pressures. It was clear now that this pastor came with a price tag.

He loved to live luxurious at the expense of the church. As he began to bankrupt the church, many of the members decided to leave. I was beginning to understand why this pastor was favoring the young deacon. The deacon would give the pastor personal love offerings and, in turn, the pastor would allow him special privileges.

With time, several members of the congregation decided not to return thereby leaving the church in a financial crisis. The pastor would often call emergency meetings with the ministers and leaders. These meetings consisted of the church's finances. Everyone was obligated to attend, and no one would be allowed to leave until the financial problems were resolved.

Every meeting he would start with: "I know that we can resolve these problems within this room." In other words, he wanted to get the money issues resolved from the ministers and leaders. At every meeting, every member would be coerced into giving one hundred dollars.

If you questioned or refused, he would then question your leadership or ministry.

It was later discovered that this pastor had caused some trouble during his time in Mexico. This had been the reason behind the associate pastor's decision to resign and congregate elsewhere. He knew the reputation the pastor had for living beyond the financial capabilities that the general assembly could provide.

The pastor at one point in his ministry was asked to supervise the churches in Mexico. He would visit the churches there and coerce them into giving him love offerings according to his financial needs. The associate pastor that resigned knew of his reputation and decided it was best for him to congregate elsewhere.

My wife's brother (who eventually married) and his wife decided to leave. He was having conflicts with the pastor's son over the decisions he was making with the musicians. Her brother was not the type of person to refrain from speaking. The pastor's son had spoken to his father about their conflicts, and my brother-in-law was asked to resign from the music ministry.

My wife wanted to leave as well but I pleaded with her to stay. I knew that if we left, I would be forced to resign and possibly lose my ministry. I had worked hard to prove I was a worthy minister.

What seemed to be a great ministry and marriage was all falling apart. We had not made it past our first year of marriage, and we were faced with so much opposition. The pressure from the pastor was intense! He was targeting me directly! The associate pastor who was now my best friend was witness to all that had been going on. He tried to remain as neutral as he could. He would encourage me to just hold on. No matter how much I tried, it was taking its toll on me.

I was getting the feeling that I was not wanted in the church.

One evening, the pastor questioned my wife's hair before the service. My wife never liked her natural brown hair color because it did not complement her light skin tone. She would color her hair black. I did not mind it! It made her feel happy and gave her confidence. One day, the color mixture was too strong and the pastor noticed the change. He called us into his office with his wife and sister-in-law present and scolded us.

In my frustration, we walked out into the hallway and I spoke harshly to her. I told her that she had embarrassed me and was costing my ministry. I broke her heart! There is no possible way to describe the look of disappointment in her eyes towards me.

She looked at me full of tears and said to me: "I'm your wife, you are supposed to be defending me!"

She left the church in that instance in tears and went home. I sat in service as long as I could, but her words were like a two-edged sword. I hurt her! I felt like a piece of trash. I left the service and went home. I apologized to her and asked for her forgiveness.

She looked at me and said she could no longer be a part of the church. She asked me if she could join her brother who was congregating at a nearby church. I agreed and committed to supporting her decision.

I would continue to congregate at the church and join her during the afternoon service where she had been attending with her brother. I did not want to resign from the ministry, so I made the sacrifice to endure the torture from the pastor. After that incident, he never asked me about my wife. I figured he was just waiting for me to leave as well.

It was exhausting after a few months! After much pleading from my wife, I eventually took a leave from the ministry and went to join her. She was happy to have me by her side, but stepping away from the ministry left a hole in my heart that would later be filled with resentment.

During my interview process for the ministry, I failed to notice why it was so important for spouses to be present and I did not understand why some couples were rejected. I began to remember my interviews for the ministry where the Bishop and the elders would ask the candidates' wives questions with regards to their faithfulness to the church and their understanding of how demanding the ministerial life could be! If the spouse was not in agreement about the ministry, the Bishop and elders sought best not to proceed with approving them for the ministry to avoid conflicts later on.

To this day, I cannot blame this pastor for the difficulties in my marriage; he was just an infuriating factor. I did not understand that there was no point in having a great ministry if I lost my spouse; I did not stand up for myself or protected my wife.

It was at this moment that I should have made some changes to strengthen my marriage regardless of my ministry, or how in love I was with the idea of marriage. I was at a fork in the road and I had to make a decision and choose a path – one that would lead me down a life of success or towards failure and destruction. As time will tell, I failed to make the proper changes.

Perhaps, I knew that I needed to make some important changes but...I did not know how. Not having a father present in my life was beginning to reflect how much I lacked the understanding of being a man and a husband.

Chapter 9

Marriage and Personal Struggles

Everyone has a story! Sometimes we fail to fully investigate how deep their story is. Maybe it's our human nature to fear digging too far into a person's life — we may not like what we find. Some people come into a relationship with openness and forthrightness; others hide their secrets well. Marriage or a commitment to marriage does not mend the scars of past emotional and psychological trauma.

Others believe that once they fall in love with a person, their past (or the past of the partner) has stayed in the past and that love will overcome all obstacles! Those that are faith-based will lean on the belief that love is the greatest force we have in this world, especially when that love is pure, and it comes from Jesus!

Christians get into problems because they never allowed Jesus into their marriage from the beginning, or they leave Him out of the problems because they fear they are sinning by bringing to Him their problems. Just because someone has given their life to Jesus or has faith, does not exempt them from marital problems, let alone divorce.

A mother bird is known for going to extreme measures to empty their nest, and make room for the next batch of offspring. The mother bird gathers her chicks and pushes them out of the nest one by one. The chick is then forced to learn how to fly, or hit the bottom and die.

I can only wonder how life would have turned out had my wife acted like the mother bird. My wife's mother had passed away when she was fifteen. Since the passing of her mother, she had grown attached to her older brother.

When I met her, I knew they were close, but somehow, I believed our marriage would be able to break that bond. I had never had a close relationship with my mother or any one of my siblings, so I did not understand how strong the bonds could be between siblings.

I had a small apartment before we married. During our engagement, we had some disagreements about how our living arrangements would be. I wanted to stay in my apartment and save money so that we could purchase a home, and she wanted to continue living with her brother.

She would argue that the apartment was too small for two people. It would have been affordable and, it would have been temporary. I was moving up in the company and so was my salary. We would have been able to purchase a home in no time. There was no need to move in with him.

Her brother worked, but was not able to pay the mortgage on his own. She wanted us to move in with him and split the cost. She calculated the expenses and stated the savings would be about the same, if we moved in with him.

The home was small but large enough to accommodate the three of us. She would always end the conversation with: "It would be temporary until he either gets married or finds a better job." It was an argument that I could not win. I was spending most of my time visiting her at her house, so in the end, she won the argument.

A few weeks before the wedding, I started to move my belongings into the home. After the wedding, I moved in and it was official.

During the wedding reception, she had asked her friend to make sure the top tier of the cake was not cut. Her family had a tradition she wanted to follow. According to the tradition, you're supposed to keep the cake in the freezer, and eat it on your first anniversary. This was meant to be a symbol of commitment. I was unaware of that tradition, but if it made her happy, I was happy! After the wedding, she put the cake into its box and put it in the freezer.

We spent a few days home after the wedding then left for Orlando to enjoy our honeymoon. Upon returning from our honeymoon, my wife wanted to cook her first official meal as a married couple so we went to the market. When we returned, I was helping her put the groceries away. She opened the freezer to make room for the items we bought and, she noticed the box with the cake missing. She asked me if I put it away somewhere. I told her I had not touched it!

She asked her brother about the cake and he laughed. He stated that we left him in the house with nothing to eat all week and in his hunger, he ate the cake. That was the first time I saw her break-down in tears. She was broken up over the missing cake! She yelled at him that he knew what the cake meant to her.

There had always been some friction between her brother and me. He was highly protective of her. He was raised in the church and he was passionate about God; but he knew underneath all the changes that God had made in me, I was a street kid. I was not trying to fool him and hide that fact from him, some things you cannot hide. Since the beginning, no matter what I did, he always made me feel like I was not good enough for his sister.

He had taken the role of not only being her older brother, but also a father figure to her. Since the passing of their mother, the family went through a difficult transition. The father had battled with depression over the death of his wife and made some poor choices. Seeing his decline, her brother decided to move to Texas taking her and the younger brother with him. When they decided to move back home, they felt they could not live in the same house with their father. It so happened that our church was in need of a musician and he was offered the opportunity. He felt it would have been a great opportunity. He accepted the position and moved.

The Latino culture is highly family oriented! It is common for family members to live together or close to each other. My family was raised in traditional American culture in that though we all lived close to each other geographically, all my aunts and uncles lived very separate lives from us.

My experience, when I was younger having nineteen people living in the house was a nightmare! I always wanted to have my privacy. I did not want my wife to think I was selfish and didn't want to help her brother; I just wanted to be on our own.

Moving into their house was a problem since the beginning. The friction between her brother and I did not help. He felt that it was his house, his rules, and his sister so he had the final word. He had a full-time job, but it was not enough for him to live independently. I was stuck!

No matter how much I pleaded with my wife that we needed to get our place, she did not want to leave him in a position that would make it hard on him. She always found a way to take his side and protect him.

Their middle brother decided to move a few months later. It was a small three-bedroom home. There was an extra room to accommodate him, but it would take its toll on our privacy. He moved in. He was a very quiet young man, and he was never a bother. Now there were four living in the house.

Seeing his sister married must have woken something up in him. He met this wonderful young lady over the internet and eventually married her. She was from Ohio. They married and he made the arrangements with her parents that she would move to Florida with him.

Her parents agreed and allowed her to move on the condition that she brings her older sister with her. She moved in and so did the sister. The sister took the middle brother's room and he slept in the living room. Eventually, the middle brother married the older sister, and they moved into the room together. Now there were six. It was constant conflict! Her brother made it clear that he was the man of the house, so his wife was now the woman of the house. My wife and her brother purchased the house together, but her brother felt that he had the right to make all the decisions.

His wife was a Black American. She loved to cook for everyone! Some days, her food was mouth-watering. On other days, she went heavy on the Soul food. I had never acquired a taste for Soul food. I would either ask my wife to make me something according to my likes or we would go out to eat. I never meant to be rude or disrespectful, she was an amazing cook.

Her brother would feel offended that I would not eat his wife's food. My wife would constantly remind me that I was being rude. No matter how much I tried to make them understand that it was not that I didn't want to eat her food, there were certain foods that I did not like, I always looked like the bad person.

I would express my frustrations about our living conditions to her, but she stated they could not afford us leaving.

Three couples living in a small house. A year had passed and things were starting to settle down. Eventually, everyone in the house had a job. The two sisters were nurses. They were able to transfer their credentials and started working. They worked in the hospital and were becoming financially stable. I felt it was time to leave! My wife struggled with the idea of having to leave. She enjoyed living close to her brothers, and she loved her sisters-in-laws. I loved them just as much, but she was not considering me.

For the first year of my marriage, I was a husband with no rights to the decisions made over his wife. It was very frustrating! I remember watching the sitcom "Full house:" Three men living in one house was ok until Jesse eventually married and had kids. Danny married, and he had his three daughters.

Joey then started feeling left out. Everyone loved him and he loved everyone, but he felt out of place! One day, they had to move him down to the basement to give him his privacy. I felt just like Joey...out of place! I would have settled for a basement, but that was not possible.

My first year of marriage was met with an abusive pastor and my wife's resistance to leave her family. There was opposition from church and at home. I do not think my wife understood all that I was going through. I knew it was not easy for my wife either. She was being targeted directly from the pastor and she had a husband that was not defending her.

The only thing that she could lean on was her brothers and their wives. The more difficult it became at church, the more drawn she was to her family. I was not much of a help to her continually pressuring her for us to move out and heed the demands of the pastor.

I do not know if my wife had ever considered how I was feeling! I had my ministry threatened by my first pastor, if I did not get married. My second pastor was threatening my ministry if my wife did not perform according to his standards without question.

My wife's decision to remain with her family was taking its toll on me. We had no privacy and it was very difficult to have intimacy freely, because of fear that any sound we made would echo throughout the house. I was not able to freely enjoy my wife!

After our first year, I finally came to my breaking point. I told my wife, either we move, or I am leaving without you. She was also feeling some of the frustrations because at times, no matter how much she loved her new sisters, she felt that she was not in her own home. She talked to her brother about our decision to move out. The house that they had purchased together was an older home and needed attention. It was not worth investing money into. They decided to sell the house and divide the profit.

My wife had been congregating with her brothers and their wives for a few months. I would attend the mornings at my church and visit the church with her family during the evenings. It was exhausting! My wife asked me if I would consider leaving the church and congregate with her and her family.

I was against leaving the church! As much as I wanted to stay, I did not have the strength to continue with such an abusive pastor, I tried encouraging myself by thinking: "The bishop will soon hear of what is going on, and have him removed." But there was no sign of him leaving.

Once the pastor found out that my wife had stopped congregating, he called me into the office to inform me that he could no longer use me in the ministry. He indirectly took my ministry away. I was not disappointed with him taking my ministry away as I was knowing as a pastor, he was hurting God's church. I decided to resign from the ministry and congregate with my wife!

After the house was sold, we found a place of our own. It would be a new start for us. We had the chance to start a new life that would involve just the two of us. We would be starting a new church together and for the first time, living on our own. It took a lot of tears and felt a lot of pain to get to this point. Things should have gotten better for us!

Even with the move, she could not break the bonds that held her to her brothers. She would spend a lot of time after work visiting them. Some days, I did not mind because I would work late. On days that I didn't work late, I would have to call her and ask her to come home to have dinner with me. I cared deeply about her brother even though there was friction. We had shared a few private moments that allowed us to create a bond. He knew I would do anything for him and his sister. I never wanted to take her away from her brother; I just wanted my wife's full attention!

Intimacy was a problem since the beginning. We did not have a problem being intimate; the problem was having privacy. Many nights, we would rush the intimacy or tried to be as quiet as we possibly could. It became a normal way for us to be intimate!

The intimacy problems followed us into our new home. We had struggled for the past year, to the point that she had gotten used to having little to no intimacy. I could not enjoy intimacy freely with my wife, even after we moved out.

After selling the house, we purchased a mobile home. There was not much profit made from the house, but we were able to afford to pay off the mobile home. She was not too happy about living in a mobile home. Her plan from the beginning was to move in with her brother and save money.

All the while we lived with her brother; we were not able to save money! For the first year, we carried most of the burden of the expenses. The mobile home was the only thing we could afford. The mobile home was not the problem; the separation from her brothers affected her. We lived close by, she was able to visit them freely, yet, it was not enough to keep her happy.

That year, the state had one of the worst hurricane seasons. It was a constant evacuation from the mobile home. Every evacuation we went to her brother's house. With every evacuation, she would find a reason to justify moving back with her brothers.

Hurricane Charley came nearby and caused minimal damage to our mobile home. She pointed out how dangerous living in a mobile home could be and we needed to move out. I could not win the argument. She convinced me to sell the mobile home!

Her brother lived in a duplex nearby. It so happened that the joining unit became available and she wanted to take advantage of the fact that it was available. We not only needed a place to stay, but we would also be moving next to her brothers.

Her brother's wife had been expecting and recently gave birth to their first child. This gave her another reason to be closer to them! Everything seemed to be falling into place for her. It was a nightmare for me!

The duplex was short-lived. They all conspired to rent a large home that would fit everyone. I was ok living next to them, I had my privacy and my wife did not have to go far to visit them. I was getting used to my wife being so close to her family, but we did not have to move in together. It didn't make sense!

The duplexes had only two bedrooms. It was fine for her brothers and their wives until the baby came. They felt the baby needed a room of her own. They all agreed on the move against my approval, and once again, we moved in together as one big happy family.

The house was large enough to give everyone some breathing room, but we were still in the same situation. Just as before, the same problems arose only in a different setting. Who was the man of the house? Who was the leader of the women? Who had the final word in the decision making?

My wife had always been used to her brother making all the decisions. He was her older brother. In my frustration, I spoke to her and let her know that I did not marry her; I married her and her family. She never understood that since the day we came home from our honeymoon, she never allowed me to grow as a man and a husband for her. I felt useless as a husband.

It was taking its toll on me. There were many nights that I did not want to come home. I would either work late, or spend more time at the church.

The pastor eventually left the church. He bankrupted the church and only twenty members remained. He did not last a full year; yet, his damages would take several years to repair.

The associate pastor, who was also my best friend, was allowed to lead the church as acting senior pastor until a replacement could be found. During the whole time of my separation from the church, I was in constant communication with him. He had been a good friend. We had been through so much under the ministry of my first pastor and now this pastor. The Bishop of the district came to our church and announced that they would be giving the senior pastor's position to him. He was excited and eager to work.

A few months after the pastor resigned, I decided on returning to the church to help him pick-up the pieces. The church was in desperate need, not only of financial support, but emotional support as well. This was my church and my family. I never stopped loving them!

My wife was supportive of the decision as well. Her brothers and their wives also agreed to come on-board to help the pastor. I was returning out of love and because I wanted to work. I did not exceed or make demands of the ministry. Her brothers were musicians and were asked to help with the music. It was a blessing to the church and them. We all found a place to help...I was returning home! The church started to experience phenomenal growth, during the first years of the pastor's ministry.

One day, the pastor called me into the office to have a meeting. He knew what my situation was, and he understood that I was not after my ministerial license. The Bishop of the district was coming to visit the church and to show his support to his new position as senior pastor, he asked me if I would consider speaking to the Bishop about my situation. He encouraged me to speak with him and see if he would grant me the privilege to return to the ministry. I discussed it with my wife and she was supportive.

The Bishop came to the church. We had a meeting and discussed all that had happened. The pastor was in the room and testified on my behalf all the wrongdoings that had taken place. He witnessed how the previous pastor, was personally targeting my wife and me. I was granted the privilege to return to the ministry. What I thought had died...was revived. There were no words to thank my pastor!

With all that I had faced over the past year and a half, I was seeing some light of hope. Moving back with her family did not seem all that bad at the moment. I prayed that things would start to turn around for us.

To this day, I often wonder if my wife was scared of letting go of her brothers. Had she built the courage to set her brothers free, we would have built a great nest together? Maybe the pain of watching her brother's fall was greater than seeing them fly on their own. Maybe she focused more on them and not enough on building her own nest.

Chapter 10

Loving and Losing

As a boy, my mother had a 1979 Ford Fairmount. She loved that car! But she eventually gave it to my brother for his sixteenth birthday. It was a fourteen-year-old car, but it drove like it was new. My brother never had any money for gas, so my mom was confident that he would not be driving much.

My stepfather, whom my mom eventually married, is a mechanic. He has always gotten after my mother for using the low-grade gasoline in her car and running it on empty. He told me once, in his frustration, that you are never supposed to use the low-grade gasoline in a car and let the gas tank run empty.

The "cheap gas," as he called it, has a lot of particles that clog the fuel injectors. He advised me in front of my mother, hoping she would listen, to only use the mid-grade gasoline and never let it run empty to avoid damaging the car's fuel system.

It turned out, my mother's Ford Fairlane, that she gave to my brother, was ruined because of my brother's carelessness in letting the car run

on gas fumes. Running the car on empty and not properly feeding it mid-grade gasoline, caused the car to have one problem after another, until it eventually gave out.

This car was fascinating! My brother would drive all around town for hours. My uncle, the mechanic, would say that the car was able to drive on gas fumes. It was amazing to see how far he was able to drive without filling it with gas. He would often make bets with his friends to see how far he could drive without running out of gas. He would drive out of town taunting his friends that they would have to push the car back home. He would win the bets, and fill his tank with gas. He was so confident in the car's fuel economy that he drove carelessly, yet confident in the car's ability to use as little gas as it did.

The car eventually gave out! The fuel pump was first to give out; then the carburetor, and eventually the car was sold for parts. For almost a year, he pushed the car to its limits running it on gas fumes for so long. The car gave all it could, and died.

There is only so much that your marriage can run on! If you feed your marriage love; if you invest time, and you allow it to grow, you will have a healthy and prosperous marriage! If you do not fill up the gas tank in your marriage and continually run it on gas fumes, it will begin to give out one part at a time until eventually, you will have no other choice but to end its life.

The Bishop had allowed me to return to the ministry. My journey over the past years had been difficult, but I never stopped loving God. God was not to blame for all that I had encountered! Even through all the trials that I had endured, I was still passionate about God, and wanted to serve Him regardless of my position. I made a promise to Him one day to serve Him, and I was holding on to that promise.

Returning to the ministry allowed me to maintain the hope that my marriage could be saved — after all, God's specialty is healing the sick, and reviving the dead. I began to dedicate my life to the ministry. This started to become my escape from all the problems that I was dealing with at home. The youth pastor, who took a leave, also returned. The pastor was beginning to have a great support team by his side as the church began its transition.

One by one, the members that had left started to return. God began to move in the church in ways that we had never experienced before. God was blessing the congregation financially and, in return, the church's finances were improving.

With only a few members in the congregation, and on the verge of losing our church building due to a lack of funds, God came through with a miracle. The pastor had been with the church a few years before me coming to the church for the first time. He was the young man that was part of the youth group but did not want to participate because he felt he was older, and did not fit in with the youth.

The acting pastor (associate pastor) was ordained into the ministry the same year I was initiated into the ministry as a deacon. He had always been a faithful member of the church and loved God passionately. God had blessed and prospered his ministry and was now using him as a pastor. It was wonderful to see what God was doing through his ministry and dedication.

The acting pastor remained faithful during the difficulties the church had passed through with the previous pastor. He had experienced three pastors' administrations in the church and was confident this most recent pastor was going to pass over, too. The acting pastor would encourage me to hang in there, but my experience with the current pastor was different than his. In the end, the acting pastor was the only minister who endured the hardship under the most recent pastor's administration.

The acting pastor had three kids at the time he became senior pastor. His wife was very loving and supportive of his ministry. The acting pastor asked the youth pastor to serve as associate pastor advancing within the church hierarchy. The three of us would spend countless hours at church planning and strategizing how to handle the new growth. The fruits of our labor were being noticed as the church was being revived.

The growth that we were experiencing had exceeded our capabilities and we could not meet the needs of the congregation because there was too much work for the three of us. We did not know how to manage such rapid growth. Some evenings, our wives would get frustrated waiting for us to finish our meetings. The associate pastor's wife was the first to tell her husband that he needed to find a ride home because she was leaving. She became tired of waiting for our meetings to finish.

The pastor's wife eventually decided to take a separate car to the church, so that she could leave right away. My wife also began to bring her car, so that she would not be waiting on her own. The three of us had our ministries rooted in the tradition that as ministers God comes first, then the church, and then our families falling behind the church.

Pentecostal's wives were meant to be submissive and supportive. During the 90's and early 2000's, there was such a demand on the ministers to be faithful to their calling, that it created friction within the family for putting the needs of the church before the needs of the family.

The church can be very demanding on its pastors, and in turn, the pastors can be demanding on their ministers, with an effort to meet the needs of the church. The weekly schedule at the church consisted of: Mondays prayer meetings, Tuesdays Bible college, Wednesday mid-week service, Thursday a rest night, Friday youth service, Saturdays consisted of some sort of fund-raising activity or district activity, and Sundays, was an eight-hour shift, which consisted of: Sunday school, Spanish service, and the evening English service.

It was overwhelming! There were other duties that included sick visits to the hospitals, meetings or counseling sessions, and invites to dinner from a member of the congregation. This did not include our jobs during the day.

The pastor had been married for ten years. The associate pastor had been married for more than fifteen years. They had their difficulties and struggles, but they had endured the trials of marriage. They were experienced men, faithful husbands, and loved the ministry. I was entering into my second year of marriage, and my roots had not been able to be firmly planted.

I prayed continuously that God would touch my wife, and allow her to see how important it was that we leave her family. The more I prayed, the more her heart was hardened. The more I prayed that she break free from the bonds of her family, the more closely she was drawn to them.

The senior pastor suggested that during the nights that we had our ministerial meetings, she should go out to dinner with the other wives. This would have been a great opportunity for her to express her frustrations to the more experienced women/wives. The Bible teaches that:

" the older women likewise, that they be reverent in behavior, not slanderers, not given to much wine, teachers of good things that they admonish the young women to love their husbands, to love their children, (Titus 2:3-4 NKJV)."

She tried on several occasions to join the ministers' wives on social activities but did not fit in; my wife felt out of place because the other wives were much older and had children. We had not been able to conceive, and hearing them talk about their children, reminded her of her struggles to conceive; therefore, she did not want to participate with them. It would have helped her to understand the demands not only as a minister's wife, but also as a woman. The absence of her mother was beginning to reflect on how she lacked the understanding of being a woman and a minister's wife.

The growth of the church and the demand for meeting its needs came at a high price. The pastor had been mentoring new members to work as local deacons help relieve the pressure, but it was not enough. The church was growing faster than we could prepare new ministers and leaders.

The growth caused a shift within the senior pastor. He began to be just as demanding as the previous pastors had been. The pastor began to demand that the ministers and leaders be present at every service, and activity! The associate pastor was having difficulties committing to all the church activities because of other non-religious commitments. When he could not commit to all that was being asked, he was asked by the senior pastor to step down as associate pastor, but remain as a minister.

I thought the associate pastor was being rebellious and did not want to commit. Maybe he did not want to be part of the church growth. I had a great relationship with him over the years. He had mentored me for a number of years so I could not understand why he would not want to be part of what God was doing in the church after all that the church had endured. I thought he was being rebellious! I did not know –until years later – that he had chosen the needs his family over the demands of the church.

I was now the associate pastor. I had not only been the youngest minister in our district, but I was also now the youngest associate pastor. I had lost contact with my first pastor, but I felt a sense of pride just knowing he would have been proud of me. Just as he was the youngest pastor within our assembly, I was bound to follow his footsteps.

While I was prospering in one area, I was losing ground in another.

The senior pastor began making more demands of my service in the ministry, now that I was the associate pastor…it was expected! I experienced the church decline and its struggles, but I had not experienced the struggles of church growth. I had been in the church for almost seven years now. I prayed that things would settle down once the church was stable, and we had more ministers.

Within time, I began to encounter the same difficulties I faced with the previous pastor. He would remind me that I was now an associate pastor, and I had to lead by example. The pastor began demanding that my wife be more of a presence in my ministry and in the church. He wanted my wife to be an example to the women in our congregation regardless of her age.

He had an idea of some of the struggles that I was having within my marriage, but he did not understand how much I had been struggling at home! I was married, but I did not feel like a husband. I was feeling less of a man because of my wife's inability to separate herself from her family. I was prospering on the outside, but dying on the inside.

I found myself once more in a situation that would bring more pressure into an unstable marriage! My wife and I never argued. We had disagreements, but we never allowed our disagreements to go further. The senior pastor began to pressure me to speak to my wife about her attendance, her attire, and her lack of involvement. My wife loved the Lord and the church. She was always willing to serve; but she made it clear, she did not want to be a slave to the church.

My wife had a passion for working with the youth! It was the one area that allowed her to minister to others freely. The youth ministry brought out the best in her. We had been down this path once before. The pastor wanted her to step away from the youth, and focus her service in other areas that would benefit me as an associate pastor. Once again, I began to speak harshly to her reminding her of her position as a pastor's wife. It caused me pain to see her in tears! I don't know what hurt her more; me not defending her, or her knowing that I cared more about the ministry than I did her?

We never had any financial difficulties during the time of our marriage. God was not only prospering my ministry, but He was also prospering me at work. I tried to love my wife to the best of my abilities. Through all of my struggles within the church and with her family, I did what was within my means to give her a good life.

I loved her the only way I knew how! She never lacked anything. It was noticeable that she had a husband that would spoil her. I felt it was the only way that I could show her how much I loved her and wanted her to be in my life! I could have given her a good home, but she refused. I wanted to give her more of me, but I couldn't. I had to share her with her family.

The more I prayed that God touch her heart, and open the door for us to move, the more she resisted! I was happy on one hand, and miserable on the other. God had anointed me with powerful ministry! He was using me to heal the sick and to bring people closer to Him.

The pastor began to rely on my ministry as his ministry grew! As God began to prosper his ministry, he would receive invites to speak at other churches within the district. In his absence, I was leading the church. There was such an anointing in the church, yet, I was miserable!

I was married, but I could not enjoy my wife freely! I struggled for years because of all the distractions, interference, and pressure. I wanted my wife to be like the wives of the senior and associate's pastors'. They had their struggles, but they were understanding and supportive. My wife was supportive in a way, but was not always by my side. She was distant.

I wanted a marriage just like those of my first pastor and the associate pastor. I would have accepted having a family like that of my childhood friend. I wanted to be married but I didn't want a marriage like the one I had. She was beginning to feel the pressure of my frustration.

I was so caught up with the idea of marriage that I failed to first; stand up for myself and fight for what I wanted; and second, to protect my wife and discover... what it was that she wanted out of the marriage. I did not stand up to my first pastor, to her brother, to the second pastor, and now, to my senior pastor who was beginning to pressure me. The pastor loved me dearly. I understood that he wanted to be successful as a pastor, but I wish I would have been able to open up to him about my personal problems. He may have offered us more guidance instead of pressure.

We had been married for three years now. I was reaching my breaking point! The constant pressure from my pastors and the constant presence of her family had taken its toll.

I pressured my wife to move out! I had expressed to her my frustrations more than enough. I explained to her that I was a husband, but I did not feel like a man. I asked her if she would allow me the opportunity to become a man and the husband that she wanted me to be. She succumbed to my request and we moved out. She was not happy, but she figured, I had sacrificed so much for her over the years, it was her turn.

She took the initiative and found a small apartment for us. It was small, but comfortable. I would have settled for another mobile home

169

just to get a chance to finally be alone with her. The apartment was in a luxurious, gated subdivision close to the beach so it gave us the feeling that we were finally moving up in the world. What I enjoyed most was that the apartment was across town from where her family was living. I was proud of her! I spared no expense to furnish the place just as she wanted. Financially, we were doing well. She had enrolled in nursing school and was working as a nurse. We needed to be on our own! It was long overdue. For the first time, I felt like a king in a palace. It was small, but it was ours.

The apartment was short-lived! Within a few months, she had met a man that was going through a divorce. His wife had left him and he did not want to stay in the house because of the memories. It was a very nice home! He wanted to rent it with the possibility of selling it, before the divorce. She encouraged me to see the home. Against my desires, I went to see the house and I fell in love with it!

This was the house in which I had always envisioned my family residing! We talked about the house for several days. I loved the house, and it was too good to pass up, but the timing did not feel right. I wanted to spend time with her and not worry about a house just yet. I had not had an opportunity to spend time with her without all of the distractions. I wanted to wait but she insisted on renting the house. We had been on our own for a few months and things were going great. I finally had my wife's full attention!

After work, she would come home to cook for us, and we would have dinner together. It was a quiet and peaceful atmosphere! We continued to struggle with our intimacy but we were making some improvements. Living with her family made it difficult to express and discover ourselves freely. We were learning how to connect with each other on a more spiritual and intimate level. I was learning what it was to truly love my wife after three and a half years.

My wife and I were finally experiencing what it felt like to be married and on our own. She had my full attention, and I had hers! We could have worked past all of our difficulties had we made the sacrifice to heal our marriage. Anything can be fixed, if you can pay attention to the warning signs indicating that something is wrong. Had we attempted to seek professional help or counseling, and committed ourselves to digging into the root of our problems, we may have had a chance to start our relationship anew.

After a few months of living on our own, my wife began to feel the absence of her family. Her brothers had moved an hour's drive south. She would visit them occasionally, but she was noticing her brother distancing himself from her as he was now married with two kids, and one on the way. She needed to be around people! I needed my privacy and my wife, but after years of not properly feeding our marriage, and only running on fumes, the first signs that things were beginning to break down were starting to show.

The weeds that we allowed to grow in our marriage were springing up, causing to choke the good seed that was finally growing in our relationship. We were at a fork in the road – once more – and we were faced with an important decision! Do we take the path that would lead us to a prosperous marriage? Or chose the path that would lead us towards destruction?

Chapter 11

Paying the Fare

Many times I have heard the story of Jonah and the whale. As a Sunday school teacher, I would teach this to the youth and relate it to being obedient. I have heard countless preachers reference the story of Jonah to make a connection with the death of Jesus and His resurrection. I had read the story several times throughout my life but it wasn't until recently that God caught my attention and allowed me to focus on a particular scripture within the story.

"But Jonah arose to flee to Tarshish from the presence of the Lord. He went down to Joppa, and found a ship going to Tarshish; so he paid the fare, and went down into it, to go with them to Tarshish from the presence of the Lord." (Jonah:1:3 NKJV).

Someone once asked me: "How do you know if it's God's will?" This is a question that can bring confusion to many people eager to receive an answer. But from my experience, if it's God's will, He will provide the means and make a way for you to obtain that which you ask for in accordance with His will. If you find yourself encountering opposition, stressed, confused, or as in the case of Jonah (paying your own fare), and end up empty-handed, you can assure yourself that it is not in accordance with God's will.

Jonah was asked to complete a simple task! Go to Nineveh and tell the people to repent or feel God's anger come upon them. God would have provided the means to get there, provided protection, and ensured that he had a safe return. Instead, Jonah found himself paying his fare to get onto a boat to run away. It is interesting how many times we get ourselves into trouble and we eventually end up paying the consequences for our own mistakes. We often take for granted that we serve a God that offers His guidance and wisdom. We want God's help yet, as humans, we insist on doing things our way. It's not until things start to go wrong when we question God and ask, "Why did He allow this to happen to us?" I remember my first pastor once preached a sermon in which he told a story of the devil sitting outside the church parking lot crying. In the story, Jesus walked over to the devil as He saw the devil crying. As Jesus walked over to see why the devil was crying, the devil looked up to Jesus with a sad look on his face because weak Christians were always blaming him for their mistakes."

As humans, we make so many mistakes, yet, never take responsibility for them. We are quick to shift the blame. We blame the devil for all the bad that happened, and we blame God for allowing it to happen. It's no wonder the devil was crying!

After years of struggling with my wife's attachment to her brothers, and with difficult pastors, we finally had a chance to work on our marriage. While we were living with her brother, I would spend as much time away from home as I could, just to avoid the thought that I lived in a house that was not my home.

For the first time, I enjoyed coming home. I would rush home just so I could meet my wife. Some days she would come home early and have dinner ready. Other days, I would rush home and bring a meal to have ready when she arrived. I enjoyed the peace and quiet. The best part, I was finally able to enjoy wearing only my underclothes around the house.

I believe that God can always fix any mess that we get ourselves into! There may be some consequences to pay for, but He can make our wrongs right. We had our moment to allow God to heal our marriage.

A young couple from the church had been dating and was planning on getting married. The young man migrated from Mexico and came to live with his father. He had a distant relationship with his father, but wanted to work on building one with him. He decided to migrate to the United States to be with his father. His father moved away, remarried and had other children when he was a good kid. A few months after his arrival, the father decided he was going to move the family to Mexico.

The young man was not able to return to Mexico, nor did he want to return because of his engagement. The young man did not have many options, and desperately needed a place to live. His situation presented my wife with an opportunity to convince me to rent the house that became available. My wife stated that we could rent a room to the young man, and as soon as he married, the couple could live with us.

My wife and I had built a friendship with the couple. They were close to our age and we were able to relate to each other. We enjoyed having another young couple in the church. We had been the only young couple since her brother moved away.

They would often come to our apartment for dinner. I didn't mind spending time with them, or having them over for dinner, the young girl was an amazing cook. I would spend time with the young man trying to encourage him to accept Jesus into his life. My wife also grew attached to the young girl. They were indirectly helping my wife detach from her brothers.

The young man reminded me of myself! It's probably why it was easy for me to connect with him. His fiancée I had known since she was a child. Her parents were one of the founders of the church. We loved them dearly!

For several weeks, she would try to convince me to rent the house. I could never win that battle! Every time she got it in her head to move, there was no convincing her otherwise. She had been so attached to being around her family, that being on her own did not seem normal. I don't know how she managed to convince me, but she did!

I cannot remember if I agreed with the intent to win her love, or if I was infatuated with the house, but I allowed myself to be placed back in a position, that I did not want to be. It was difficult for me to convince her that we needed to move out of her brother's house and we finally did. Now, she wanted to move in with another couple! I loved the couple, and I would have been happy to have them live with us until they were able to be on their own, had it been under different circumstances. I was on our honeymoon with my wife and yet we would soon be sharing a house with another couple. The young man was facing a difficult situation and I wanted to help him so we decided to break the lease and move into our new home.

The young man was not a bother — he would work during the day and spend his evenings with his fiancée at her parents' home. I was able to hire him as one of my employees and he turned out to be a very hard working young man. He paid his share of the rent on time and he was very clean.

The lease agreement on the apartment required that we commit to a full year. If we decided to break the lease early, it would come at a high cost; we would have to pay three months' rent as well as losing the security deposit. On the new house, we then had to pay for the first and last month, plus the security deposit. We had been living in the apartment only for a couple of months before purchasing the house at my wife's insistence.

Like Jonah, we paid a high fare for getting onboard.

My wife and I were trying to adjust to another change, but something felt out of place. There was an uncomfortable feeling in the house...almost like an inexplicable sense of uneasiness.

Something was not right! One night, I came home and she was not home. I thought she may have gone out shopping. I made dinner and ate. I had a strange feeling something was out of place. After dinner, I went into the bedroom only to find a note on the bed. She had packed up her belongings and went to live with her brother. I cannot say that it was without warning. There had been plenty of warning signs since before we married. I tried calling her but she would not answer. I went to her brother's house, only to be met with an angry giant.

I could not understand what was going on or why she would do this. If she was not happy at the house, it was her idea to move there in the first place. I would have been ok with moving out and living on our own. I would have even been ok moving back with her brother because there was always a spirit of peace and love in the house when we lived together as a family! We were loved by God, so there was always prayer and praise in the house.

Her older brother eventually came around to accepting me, but there was still some tension, (the battle of alpha males). I loved and respected him, as he eventually responded in like. However, there was always conflict with the sisters-in-law either because of the cooking or cleaning; there was crying from the babies and almost never any peace and quiet.

I would go every day for the first two weeks trying to talk to her. I would wait in the parking lot praying that God would help me! One evening, her brother became annoyed with my persistence. He told me that she needed some time to herself. He assured me she was in good hands and they would be praying for the both of us. It was comforting, but I just wanted to know…what I did that was so wrong?

I can admit that I may not have been the best husband to her, but I loved her to the best of my abilities. I never expected more than she could offer. I never forced her to do anything, and I was never abusive. Although I was a workaholic and I spent most nights at the church, she knew I was faithful to her. I always dedicated my Saturdays to her and Sundays we were in church together.

I could not love her any more than she allowed me to. The short time we spent together in our apartment, I was starting to discover a deeper and more passionate love towards her. I did not understand, I just needed to know why she left!

She stayed with her brother for about a month. I was heartbroken! I was miserable the whole time she was with her brother. As I came to an empty house every night, all I could do is think! The more I thought, the more resentful I became.

I began to remember the words she said to me, the night we talked about our relationship: "I am aware of what the ministerial life is; my mom was a pastor's wife. I witnessed what she had to endure. I will support you, and I would love to be a part of your ministry." Why would she do this?

For the first week, I went on a spiritual-warfare attack on the devil. He was the one trying to ruin our marriage and my ministry. I prayed and fasted like never before. After seeing no results, I began to question God. "Why was He allowing us to go through this?" I would also question God, and ask Him, "Why didn't He protect my wife?" I didn't get a response from God either.

As much as it pained me, I gave her time and space. I did not call or seek her. I would send her a text message every now and then just to ask if she was ok and made her aware that if she needed anything not to hesitate to contact me. After a month, she called me asking if it was ok for her to come home. I let her know this was her home and she did not have to ask for permission. She came home a few hours later and we talked.

I never hated her family, much less didn't ever want to be around them. I loved them! They were my family as well. My issue was never her brother; I just wanted my wife all to myself. She knew that I never minded her visiting them or them coming over. At one point, the brothers-in-law moved to Florida to be closer to their kids. They were very loving people, and powerful Christians. Their parents were everyone's parents. Their son, moved down too as well and he became my friend and employee. I am grateful that her family encouraged her to talk to come home and talk to me. It was her brother who told her that she either had to talk to me about her issues or find a way to end the marriage.

I anxiously waited for her to come home. She was only gone for a month, but it seemed like forever. She came home and we sat down to talk. It was hard for her to open up! All she did was cry and wanted me to hold her. I embraced her and assured her whatever the problems were, we would be ok.

She began to explain that she felt abandoned and lonely! She told me that I was always working or at church, and she hated being so far from her family. I let her know that I felt the same. I explained to her that I was tired of always living with people and I never got to enjoy her as a wife. I never wanted to take her away from her family; I felt I never had her completely. She apologized for leaving and I asked her for forgiveness for being absent.

We agreed that we would get a place of our own and try and spend more time together. She agreed not to let anyone interfere in our marriage, and I agreed to stand up for her regardless of the position they were in. I agreed to stop working so much, and spend less time at the church. We asked each other for forgiveness and we prayed for God's help.

We began to look for a place to stay as we both felt uncomfortable in the house. I discussed our decision with the young man and agreed to give him some time to save money. Things worked out for them after their wedding. They decided to move in with her parents. We found a small house and moved out. We both wanted a fresh start in our marriage.

My wife and I had been friends for nearly two years before getting married. We dated for a few weeks and were engaged for a year. Counting our friendship and engagement, we had known each other for three and a half years. We were now a few months past our fourth year of marriage. Since the beginning, our friendship was constantly being pressured, our engagement faced many challenges, and our marriage got off to a bad start. Up until then, we had always tried our best to work past our differences.

After we moved into our new place, we began having trouble adjusting to one another. In six months, we would be reaching our fifth anniversary. I remembered the words someone said to me: "If you can make it past your fifth year of marriage, your marriage would turn out to be strong, and you would be able to endure many years together."

I could only pray that we would be able to make it to our fifth year. I was confident if we made it past the fifth year, things would eventually get better for us. The more we tried to connect, the more distance was created. I tried to connect physically and intimately with her, only to be met with rejection. I tried to connect emotionally with her, only to be treated with indifference.

It turned out, there had been much more damage than I was aware of. We had begun to pay for our mistakes!

It was her turn not to want to come home. She began to spend more time with her friend, the wife of the young man that we rented the room. Her behavior was starting to change. She would go out and come home smelling of alcohol. She stepped down from her position on the worship team and eventually made excuses not to attend Sunday school and would only attend the service.

I would find receipts from restaurants that we would never dare go into. The charges were for alcoholic drinks. She started having "Get-a-ways," with her friends. It started with a one night, then two nights which eventually turned into weekend get-a-ways. She would leave Friday and return Sunday evening.

She had always managed the finances in the relationship. I was at the height of my financial success! Between both incomes, we had no financial worries. I began to notice that our bills were not being paid, and our vehicles were threatened with repossession. When I questioned her, she replied that it was a mistake and she would fix it.

I never questioned her. Not about her weekend get-a-ways or the drinking. I never accused her of being unfaithful. I always said to myself, "I would never do something that I would not want done to me!" Several times during the course of our relationship, I mentioned to her that if she was ever unhappy with me, please let me know and we would either find a way to fix our problems or end our relationship. I trusted her. I could never imagine her being unfaithful. She loved God!

October of 2008, I received notice that I was being laid off from my place of employment. I had seen it coming and it was just a matter of time. The country had been facing a financial recession and we were seeing a decline in orders. Little by little, the company was having waves of lay-offs until the company decided to close for good. All the employees received the notice on a Thursday morning, and were given the option to finish off the day.

I chose to finish the day thinking it would be a day's pay. My drive home was difficult! I did not know how I was going to tell my wife. I was unsure if I should tell her right away or wait until

Sunday. I did not want to hide anything from her so I decided to tell her! I was broken over the incident, yet, she did nothing to comfort me. Honestly, I expected her to at least tell me it was going to be alright! She asked me if I was hungry. I was not in the mood to eat, but she said she was hungry and asked me to join her for dinner. We went to dinner and she ate while I poked at my food. It was an awkward feeling. I just sat there with a depressed countenance. She just spent the time on her phone.

The drive home was no better; she did not say a word. She had been indifferent to me for some time. In a way, I was hoping she would have shown me some form of support. I would have settled for any words of encouragement. "We will be fine, don't worry, God's in control, we will manage." She had a look on her face as if she was in deep thought, but she would not speak.

We arrived home and I went straight to the bedroom. I wanted to spend some time alone just to clear my head. She came over and sat next to me. For a split second, I thought she was going to give me a hug. She said she wanted to tell me something. I sat up trying to muster up a smile awaiting some good news.

To my surprise, she wanted to confess something to me that she had been withholding for some time. She paused for a moment as the tears ran down her face. She told me the reason she had left to stay with her brother a few months ago was that she had an affair. She felt devastated over what she did, and in her guilt, she left! She had confessed to her brother and his wife what she had done.

Her brother was disappointed with her but was supportive. He encouraged her to confess to me what had happened and to try and work things out with me. She never confessed what she had done and tried to shift her guilt towards my absence. She had an affair and did not want to own up to her mistake and thought she could somehow hide her mistake.

I should have picked up on the warning signs when she was telling me that she was lonely and felt abandoned. I was too naïve to believe she was capable of being unfaithful. She said there was more. For the past two years, she had been involved in an affair. She did not say whether it was with the same person or someone else. She had decided that she was going to end our marriage and was going to live with him.

She had her bags packed in the spare bedroom we had. She had planned on leaving with him in the morning while I was at work. She gave me the note that she had written and was going to leave it on the pillow. Since I no longer had a job, she had no choice but to confess! She expressed that she cared deeply for me, but she was not "In Love" with me. I asked what her plans were, now, that she confessed everything to me. She asked me if I could take her to her friend's house with her bags, and he would pick her up from there.

She was texting him during dinner that evening that their plans had to change because she could no longer run away in the morning. She started to cry and told me that this was not the life that she wanted. She was tired of all the criticism, tired of being alone, and tired of being called a "pastors wife." She told me how I never stood up for her when she needed me to. She felt like a wife with no husband!

With all that she was saying, the only thing that echoed through my head were her words: "I know what the ministerial life is, my mom was a pastor's wife, I will support you and I want to be a part of your ministry." I was not angry with her. Disappointed? I was very disappointed with her! I would have preferred that she ended our marriage instead of committing to an adulterous relationship for the past two years. Of all the days she could have chosen to confess, why today?

The ship sailing to Tarshish finally received their payment in full from the both of us. In the end, we both were putting money into the savings account that would later serve to pay the fare. The fare was long overdue, and it came at a high price! I gathered her belongings and put them in the car. I drove her to her friend's house where to my surprise; the affair partner was waiting for her. It was strange why she decided to introduce him to me. The young man reached out to shake my hand. I told him I was sorry, but I could not shake his hand. I unpacked her bags and drove back home. It had been years since I last experienced what I had been used to — losing everything I had come to love!

I came back home and wrote my pastor, and the Bishop a letter of resignation. I knew I would have to eventually step down from the ministry; there was no sense in waiting. I knew I could not pay the mortgage and the bills, so I asked my mother if I could move in with her. I sold what I could and gave away what I couldn't. I packed my belongings and left.

Before Sunday ended, I lost: my job, my wife, my home, and my ministry. In the end, the pain did not come from her unfaithfulness; it came from her broken promise! No matter how much I wanted to be angry with her, I couldn't! I cannot justify her actions and behavior, she will have to discuss that with God, yet, I cannot blame her for what she did.

Adultery is unacceptable! God speaks harshly about it in the Bible, yet, I am a firm believer that there is a reason, and a root cause, as to why someone would choose to commit adultery? I do not believe in or encourage divorce. I do believe that a couple can recover and heal from infidelity.

Before I dropped off my wife at her friend's house, I confessed to her that I had been unfaithful to her as well. I was unfaithful to her not with another person, but with my job and ministry. I chose my occupations over her. I asked her for forgiveness and pleaded with her to stay and allow us to seek out help. I offered to resign from the ministry and find a less demanding job. She only cried and told me that she had stopped loving me long ago. She found someone who can love her the way she wanted to be loved. Her decision was made.

I spent the next couple of months depressed over all that had happened. The holidays were around the corner and I was miserable. Only those that have been victims of adultery will know the damage that infidelity can leave on a person. It would take me years to recover!

It turns out; Christians are not exempt from marital problems… much less divorce! After the holidays passed, I gathered my savings and contracted a lawyer to start the process of divorce. The lawyer stated the divorce could be finalized within two weeks, if I was able to get the papers filled out along with the notarization. The problem would be getting her to sign the papers.

I contacted her and let her know that I had the divorce papers ready for her to review and sign. I made it clear that I was not asking for anything and I would assume all the debt. I just wanted a peaceful divorce from her and I wanted her to be happy. I did not want to embarrass her by having the papers served to her at her place of employment, so I asked if it would be ok for me to take them to her.

I met her at a notary and we signed and notarized the papers. I told her within two weeks we would be divorced, and that she did not have to be present at the court hearing. She was surprised as to why I was pushing for a quick divorce. She once again shifted the blame and asked me what my motives where for a rapid divorce. My response was simple, "you are living with your affair partner!" There was nothing left to keep this marriage going. The papers were turned in and the divorce was finalized within weeks.

At the time, I had not heard of such a thing called, "Marriage Restoration," or "Standing for your Marriage." I was never made aware that there was an option to fight for my marriage. Even Jonah was given a second chance after his disobedience.

I never sought any counseling or asked my pastor for advice. I believed that her decision of going to live with her affair partner meant that our marriage had ended. I should have sought counseling instead of a lawyer. I never asked God if it was His will for me to divorce her. I was merciless. I had committed just as many mistakes as she did. I was just as guilty as she was.

Chapter 12

Dealing with Resentment and Bitterness

King David is known for being a great king chosen from God. "But now your kingdom shall not continue. The Lord has sought for Himself a man after His own heart, and the Lord has commanded him to be commander over His people, because you have not kept what the Lord commanded you," (1Sam. 13:14 NKJV). He wrote the majority of the Psalms and is known as being one of the greatest Kings in Israel. The Bible describes King David as being a man after His own heart, yet, he was a man with many flaws.

His fame of being a great king is also connected with one of his most noticeable failures; his decision to take another man's wife, and then having the husband killed in battle. I could spend hours writing pages and explaining how great his sin was, but I would like to redirect your attention to a different side of the story.

Uriah was the husband of Bathsheba with whom King David had an affair. The King was informed that Bathsheba was married, yet, he called her into his house. Depending on the Bible version that you are reading, the King's actions with Bathsheba were recounted differently yet with similar outcomes. One version translates that he slept with her; another is straight forward stating that he had sex; and, others that he simply went into bed with her. Regardless of how the story is translated, no version describes how Bathsheba may have felt.

The Bible gives us an insight to the character of Uriah. He was a servant and a dedicated high ranking soldier. Uriah was an honest, simple man. The Bible states that after King David had slept with his wife, she became pregnant. The King tried to cover up his sins by calling Uriah home from the battle field, hoping he would go home and sleep with his wife. Uriah instead chose to sleep outside the palace in the courtyards to protect the king. He was a man that went beyond the call of duty.

It is not mentioned in the Bible but Uriah had a mother, a father, and probably brothers and sisters. He may have been an uncle, a cousin, and someone's best friend. We are only left to wonder: did Uriah's family know that the King had murdered their family member? Perhaps, to cover up yet another sin, the King could have shifted the blame on the fact that Uriah was a soldier. It is hard to imagine what Uriah's family was thinking or feeling. Did the family blame Bathsheba for committing adultery causing the King to have her husband killed?

We know little about Bathsheba or her motives. Was she madly in love with her husband? Was she lonely and desperate for affection? Was she forced to sleep with the King? Or was she provoking him with the intent to catch his attention and willing to sleep with him? We can only wonder!

I am almost confident that she felt hatred directed towards her. Did Uriah's family hate her? Was she despised by the other wives the king had? Did all the servants in the palace enjoy the novella and gossiped about her. I am sure she was labeled as the woman who almost ruined the kingdom?

There were many people angry with my ex-wife because of her unfaithfulness. Members of the congregation would tell me that I was better off without her. My family members would tell me that if they saw her in the streets, they would do something physically to her or her car. I had friends tell me that she would end up in hell because, God makes it clear, adulterers cannot enter into heaven.

I do not remember what was worse: her confession of having a two-year affair or the sympathy I was getting from everyone. The divorce was difficult! With so many people giving me sympathy and motives to hate her, they did not realize that I was on an emotional roller coaster. I did not know whether to be happy that I was free from an adulterous woman; sad because my wife left with another man, angry because I was too naïve to know of her two-year affair, or hurt because I offered my forgiveness and would have accepted her with her mistakes and she refused.

I often wondered what she was going through. Was she battling with the shame and guilt of her sins? Did she feel rejected and ashamed before the members of the congregation and our

191

friends? Was God speaking to her about the seriousness of her sins? I know she must have had strong feelings for the affair partner and possibly loved him, but was she really happy?

We had been great friends for two years before we were engaged. We enjoyed talking to each other and hanging out with the rest of the youth group. I liked her as a friend and there were some feelings towards her, but I knew deep inside that I was not ready for marriage.

The feelings I had towards her were more on the level of friends. I was not in love with her when I asked her to marry me. At one point during my engagement, I could not help but wonder if it was God's will that we marry because the pastor and the congregation had been praying for me (many times publically) that God would send me a wife.

She showed up a year later. Maybe this was indeed the woman that God had prepared for me. It may have been that she was the person that God wanted in my life, but I (we) rushed His plans. The pressure was so immense that I could not fight it! I wanted the pressure to stop, and it prompted the both of us to rush into marriage. We liked each other's company but only as friends...platonically.

I did not allow myself more time to enjoy her more as a friend and less during our engagement. As friends, there were feelings but those feelings were not mature enough to marry. If I would have allowed myself more time, those feelings would have matured into love, and that love would have matured into a strong bond.

I would have liked to have known what her thoughts were about going into marriage with me. Was she caught up with the idea of being married to a minister just as her mother? Was she infatuated with having the young, handsome minister, as a boyfriend or possible husband? Was she pressured into engaging into a relationship with me? What taunts me the most is, did she ever love me going into the marriage?

Was she in love with the idea of marriage as well? Did she dream of having a sitcom marriage and family? Did she desire to have a family like the pastor? I would have liked to know what family values influenced her to want to marry and have a family.

If I had the ability to go back in time, I would correct many of the mistakes that I made. I would never say that I wouldn't have chosen her as a wife again, if she was sent from God, then I would be going against His will. I would have stood up for myself and stood firm on the fact that I did not want to get married. I wanted to enjoy the ministry!

I wanted to dedicate my time to serving the church, and traveling! Maybe I would have matured more into a man and I would have been able to defend not only myself but my wife when pressured by the pastors to behave in a way that fit their mold and not her nature.

Honestly, my love for Jesus was growing, and I was not fully matured as a Christian. I was passionate about serving Jesus, but my love for Him was still in its infancy. I needed more time to mature as a Christian to build a solid foundation of faith, before I started a relationship with another person.

We can all fill our lives with all the "what if's…" but no matter how much we replay in our minds all the events that took place, there is nothing that we can do to change what has already happened. Just stop and think, what was running through King David's mind after God exposed his sin? What if he would have spent time with his family instead of looking at his neighbor? What if he would have been at church praying more, he would have heard the words: "She is the wife of Uriah," more clearly! How would things have changed if he had slept with one of his wives to satisfy his sexual needs?

Psalms 51, according to scholars was written a year after the incident. Even after a year, he was devastated by his decision. The only thing left in our power is to learn from the mistakes we make. We have no control of how long the reminder of the pain we caused in others or ourselves will last or when we will heal from those mistakes.

I had chosen to forgive my ex-wife since the first day she confessed her affair; I did not allow my life to be consumed by hate. I made a choice that I was not going to hate her. That decision opened a door for me to encounter resentment and bitterness for the next ten years!

Someone made a comment to me once that left me intrigued for several years: "God will not bless a marriage built from adultery." People can be cruel!

I am against divorce, and I do not justify anyone's reasons for having an affair, besides, the bible states clearly:

"Do you not know that the unrighteous will not inherit the kingdom of God? Do not be deceived. Neither fornicators, nor idolaters, nor adulterers, nor homosexuals, nor sodomites," (1Cor. 6:9 NKJV).

I am not going to defend or condone anyone for the choices they made. I made choices of which I was not proud. To this day, I question myself if I rushed the divorce process just as quickly as I rushed the marriage. I say that I was not ready for marriage, could it have been that I was not ready for divorce either?

According to the Bible, King David committed adultery with Bathsheba, vice versa, yet, God blessed them with a son who later would inherit his father's kingdom, and become the wisest man the world had ever known. David had to face countless consequences as a result of his sin. His worst consequence would come in the form of a generational curse that would hinder many kings to come.

This is not a green light for someone to go and commit adultery. I am standing firm in that I do not justify anyone's reason for committing adultery. There is a root cause as to why people often enter into an adulterous affair. Reasons that only the individual and God know.

As humans, we can be very judgmental and hate someone for hurting us or for hurting a family member, but we never understand the reasons behind their decision to be unfaithful.

As strange as it may sound, I do not blame my ex-wife for the decision she made to step outside the bonds of marriage. She will have to discuss her decisions one day before God as we will all have to, but I do not blame her. We never allowed our marriage to be planted firmly. Because of the constant opposition, our roots were not dug deep.

I mentioned to my ex-wife on several occasions, that I felt like a husband that had to ask permission to be with his wife. I wanted her all for myself, but I had never gotten the chance. As a child, I would get into physical fights to defend my siblings. I was never afraid of losing or getting hurt, as long as my family was safe. I do not know why I was so afraid to defend my wife. I loved my first pastor, I loved my ministry, and I loved the idea of being married, but could it have been that I did not love my wife enough to defend her?

I could only imagine what it was that drove her into the arms of another man. Was I not being attentive to her needs? She had discussed with me on one occasion that our sexual life needed improvement, but I was so used to not having an intimate life, that I could not see any way of improving what we were not doing. We almost never had any privacy to be free in that area. I was too naïve to understand she was reaching out to me. She probably felt she had a husband who was not man enough to take care of her needs.

I never made an effort to consider what she wanted in life and what was it that made her happy. I had showered her with gifts throughout our marriage, but she was not interested in gifts. I worked hard to give her a good life, but she was just happy being around her family. No matter what I did, I could not do enough to win her heart.

In the end, we both are to blame for a marriage that failed. To place the blame solely on her would not be fair. There were many warning signs, even before we married, that something was out of place. I failed to notice that either God was telling me to wait, or that she was not the person whom He had prepared for me.

Even after our marriage, God was still working with the both of us trying to make the best He could with the decisions that we made. He allowed us an opportunity to revive our marriage when we finally moved out and away from her family. We cannot blame God for not saving our marriage. Did the devil come in and ruin our marriage? He is an opportunist — he saw an open door and he took it. It just so happened that my ex-wife was the weaker one in the marriage and allowed herself to fall prey. It could have easily been me who could have fallen.

If you are faith-based, you will always hear the Bible verse quoted so often: *"Therefore what God has joined together, let not man separate*, (Mark 10:9 NKJV)." If you are reading this and are not a believer, you will often hear the phrase: "If you love something and it was meant to be, it will return."

For years, I questioned if my marriage was God sent. Did I force my marriage? I never forced her to marry me, and I most certainly never pressured her to marry me as the pastor and the congregation did.

After learning that my wife had been unfaithful to me, I wondered what had moved her in that direction instead of reaching for me. Was my ex-wife a victim of her lover who was an opportunistic, just as Bathsheba fell prey to King David, looking to meet a need outside of marriage? There is little to know about Bathsheba. We can only wonder how she allowed herself to be placed in a situation where the King would have noticed her. Was she feeling lonely and vulnerable? Did she feel abandoned? Was she tired of living on the lower social status, and desired wealth and fame? Was she bored with the monotonous sex from her husband, and desired a more passionate sex life? Was she seeking something more than just being a wife... or was she simply at the wrong place at the wrong time?

Not much is mentioned about Uriah. We can gather fragments of his life such as that he was very dedicated to his job; he would spend days and maybe months away from home attending to his calling. We know that he was given a chance to come home to be with his wife but instead of enjoying the time with his wife, he ignored her to attend to his job. Was I just like Uriah, given plenty of signs that something was wrong, but ignored every warning sign?

I can only imagine that he wanted to make his wife proud, and felt he was doing the best he could for his family. He probably wanted the King to notice his dedication with the hopes of being promoted. Maybe this way, he would have been able to provide his wife a better life than what was currently within his means. The promotion could have meant that he could have spent more time strategizing in meetings closer to home and not fighting long days in the battle field.

There are always two sides of a story. There is no sense blaming the spouse that made a mistake if you do not understand the root cause of their decisions. You cannot justify adultery, but you can understand what drives them to commit that sin. There is no way to describe the pain adultery causes. It hurts! Do victims of adultery have the right to be angry with the spouse? Most certainly they do! Should forgiveness be an option? Yes, it should! What about the affair partner?

I remember years ago when my brother slept with my girlfriend. I could not be angry at my brother, what was the point? He was opportunistic! He saw an opportunity and he took it! The problem was with my girlfriend. We were in a relationship and she made a choice that would end our relationship.

There was no sense in being angry towards my wife's affair partner; victims of adultery will often get upset with the affair partner, when in the end, the problem was between the husband and the wife.

Let go and let God deal with the affair partner. He did with King David!

For years, I had said to myself that I had forgiven my ex-wife. To a certain extent, I did forgive her, but my life had been full of bitterness and resentment. For the next ten years, her words echoed continually in my head: "I know what the ministerial life is, and I am going to support you." I was constantly reminded of how much she had lied to me!

One day, I was attending a conference. During the alter call, one of the pastors came towards me as he felt moved to come and speak words of life into me. The words spoken over me that day impacted me in a manner that would begin to change my life!

The pastor, being led by the spirit, draws near and said to me: "Brother, your life is full of resentment and bitterness because of the loss of your ministry. God is going to restore your calling!" The spirit of God came upon me, and I broke down in tears.

For weeks I pondered on those words. I took them to heart as God was the only one who knew what was buried deep in my heart. Losing my ministry was painful. My pastor was very supportive of my decision to end my marriage and always offered his support. He would continue to use me as a minister at the local level and always encouraged me to grow spiritually. The church was always supportive and respected me as a minister as well. I just could not get over the loss. I mourned for years the loss of my ministry.

As I sought God's presence and asked Him what He was trying to tell me, weeks later, He gave me the revelation and I began a new journey. I was so bitter over the loss of my ministry, that it caused my relationship with God to be hindered for years, even while faithfully ministering to others. God was still blessing me! He blessed me with a wonderful wife and a son. My finances and employment was prospering, yet; I had a life full of bitterness. I was miserable. God wanted to release all the hurt, bitterness, and resentment from my life. It would be a long process!

He began to reveal areas in my life that I needed to bring to Him. As I sought His presence more, He began to show me the steps I needed to take to be released from all the bitterness and resentment. Some days, it felt like God was punishing me for all the wrong that I had done. Others were full of peace as I would begin an internal healing.

A few months later, I was able to contact my ex-wife through social media. I asked if she would allow me to send her an email. She asked to know what I was going to send. I wanted to email her a letter asking for her forgiveness and to apologize for what all that had happened.

She said: "We have already asked for forgiveness, and there was no further need to continue hindering each other with the subject." I pleaded with her. I informed her that God had burdened me over the way we handled our marriage and divorce. I was able to convince her and she allowed me to send her an email.

In my letter nine years later, I poured out my heart! Years ago, I had said to myself that I was going to forgive her and that I wasn't going to allow hate to ruin my life. The truth was there was still a lot of hate in my heart towards her. I hated her for ruining my life: I blamed her for my financial burdens; I blamed her for losing my job;

I hated her for everything I lost, house, cars, and savings. I hated her most because, while she was with her affair partner "living in sin," she was living a wonderful life while I was in financial ruins and feeling emotional betrayal and abandonment. She had her job, she had money, they would travel, and she was happy.

I was miserable and suffering! I resented her for years and it grew into bitterness. I had to move in with my mom. I was on government assistance and receiving unemployment checks. My car was repossessed by the bank, and I was lonely.

After being spoken over by the pastor, I had realized that the story was not as I had always told it. She had not ruined my life; I had ruined hers.

I married her knowing that I was not ready and I was not fully in love with her. I felt that marrying her might provoke love to grow within us and it would unite us more as a couple. I believed that I was doing the will of God and I would be rewarded with a family like that of my pastors. God could most certainly have blessed my marriage but my motives were wrong. I was seeking a sitcom marriage more than I was seeking a Godly marriage.

I explained to her that I finally came to understand that everyone makes their own choices, and everyone has to deal with the consequences of their choices. I felt it was an injustice blaming her for being an adulterer when she was seeking to be loved. I knew that I was not the person who could love her as she desired to be. I loved her as best I could, but I loved other things much more than her.

I was in love with the church, the ministry, and in love with the idea of marriage. I poured my heart out in that letter asking her forgiveness. I know I did not ruin her life completely; after all, she made her own choices. It was her decision to marry me!

Had I had the courage to stop the wedding, she could have found a more suitable partner for marriage and perhaps had the love for which she longed. On the other hand, if we had waited to marry, we could have given our relationship the time needed for a firm foundation, our marriage would have stood a chance. We could have prayed about all the opposition we were facing and waited for an answer! If we would have spent more time in the church together before marriage, we could have heard the voice of God telling us if we were meant for each other till death do us part.

I ran into her about a year later at a conference. I saw her and felt compelled by the Spirit to approach her and hug her. She had been expecting a little girl. I was happy for her as she longed to have a child when we were married, but God had not allowed us. I do not know if I was happier seeing her reconciled with God or that she was expecting. I blessed her, and thanked her for allowing me to be a small part of her life!

Chapter 13

Digging In

The Bible tells us about an incident that happened with Abram (this is the name that Abraham went by before God came into his life). In the book of Genesis, Abram was called out of his father's house and was ordered to go to a land that God would bestow on him. Somewhere in the journey, they ended up in Egypt. While in Egypt, Abram lies and tells the Egyptians that his wife Sarai (this was Sarah's name before the encounter with God) was his sister. Pharaoh takes her as his wife and God eventually brings her back to Abram, "The princes of Pharaoh also saw her and commended her to Pharaoh. And the woman was taken to Pharaoh's house, (Gen. 12:15 NKJV)." When she returned to Abram, I can only imagine Abram questioning Sarai for days whether or not she slept with the Pharaoh, or the things she was obligated to do.

There are several questions that we can spend hours debating (did Pharaoh sleep with Sarai, what was Abram doing in Egypt, why did Abram lie in the first place, etc.). I would like to shift your attention away from Abram and focus on Sarai his wife. How did the incident affect Sarai as a person?

Whether Pharaoh did or did not sleep with her, she was taken against her will. She could have spent days, if not weeks, angry with Abram for taking her to Egypt in the first place. I can only imagine the trauma Sarai felt. Had there been licensed mental health counselors available, she would have had to see one.

You can almost sense her frustration and bitterness when the angel of the Lord came to speak with Abram about his son to be borne by Sarai. "Therefore Sarah laughed within herself, saying, "After I have grown old, shall I have pleasure, my lord being old also? (Gen. 18:12 NKJV)." After the birth of her son Isaac, God changed her name and thereby started a process of spiritual transformation. Now she was no longer Sarai, but would be Sarah in Hebrew it meant "princess." Likewise God changed Abram's name to Abraham, meaning "father of nations," starting a spiritual transformation.

I believe that the spiritual transformation of Abraham and Sarah shifted their marital discord so they could raise Isaac and lead a nation in keeping with their new mission. It is difficult to deal with the trauma that is created from infidelity or divorce without external assistance to create a change or transformation to allow the relationship to heal. It is even more difficult when someone has brought their past trauma into a new marriage causing conflicts within the marriage.

I believe that God can fix any marriage! I do not promote divorce by any means. If you are faith-based, God is a God of resurrection! He can bring life to a marriage that has died. There is a great amount of damage that can result from infidelity or divorce but a marriage can be healed if the couple can receive the proper help whether it is seeking spiritual help from God through a church or through counseling and a good support system. There are many changes and sacrifices that will be required but a marriage can be saved nonetheless.

God often gives us plenty of warning signs within our marriage so that we can make the necessary changes to prevent damages. The problem is couples have to be sensitive to the voice of God and allow Him to speak and to show us where we need to make changes, whether within ourselves or within the marriage. He will also show you the challenges that your spouse may be encountering but only if you allow Him to do so. The problem often stems because we think we

know what's best and we try to do everything on our own…and never allow God into our problems.

It can take years of therapy to help you discover the root of the problems. Often times, the problems do not come from the other spouse, but from you. I had trauma created within me from the constant pressure of my first pastor and the congregation who followed, but it would be unfair to blame them for the decisions that I made. I allowed the trauma and pressure into my marriage and I was coming into a marriage full of uncertainties.

I had come to learn years later that just because someone gives their life to Jesus, it does not mean that their lives are brand new without prior emotional baggage which still needs to be sorted out. Accepting Jesus into your heart and accepting to be baptized in the name of Jesus washes away your sins but you still have to deal with your sinful nature. Walking now in the faith allows you to live a life more cautious of your choices and creating different patterns that serve your new faith in God resisting the temptation to return to your old lifestyles.

Yes! You now have Jesus to help you identify and overcome those traumas, but they are present all the same. When God freed the Israelites from Egyptian slavery, God had to spend time with them trying to get Egypt out of their minds and heart. For forty years, the Israelites were in the desert because God was trying to remove four hundred years' worth of trauma from the people.

I have spent years in the ministry speaking with couples who have experienced a situation similar to mine. There are countless couples on the edge of divorce asking: "What went wrong?" These couples felt they were doing everything they could to have a successful marriage, yet, were facing divorce.

Many couples who experienced difficulties or are going through them in their marriage, have often been the result of one spouse having a better understanding of the concept of marriage, while the other was "in love" with the idea of marriage. Often, the spouse, who has no concept of what marriage involves, tends to work harder in the marriage to achieve their ideal marriage without working together towards the same goal. While the one who understands the concept of marriage will often be the one trying to slow the other down so that they do not get too far ahead and lose each other in the process.

There are many expressions of love and many ways to show someone you love them, but these often can be confusing. "I know that I love my spouse; I want to show them that I love them, but how do I do it in a way that does not always involve intimacy?" Men tend to be more physical and think sexual intimacy with the wife is the best way to express the love they feel for them; while women feel they need to be emotionally intimate with their husband so that he feels loved. There has to be a balance in the levels of intimacy that each spouse requires be it of a sexual nature or more non-sexual.

To achieve that balance in intimacy one should look to other sources for help. Dr. Gary Chapman wrote a book entitled; "The 5 Love Languages" that has helped many people understand the needs of their spouse and how to fill those needs.

In the case of my ex-wife, she only had brothers and had difficulty relating to other women. It had been difficult for her – as a woman – not having her mother in her teenage years when she would have been developing as a woman. I failed to see that being around her sisters-in-law allowed her to identify herself as a woman and to learn from them through interaction. On the other hand, I came from a large family full of drama and chaos and as a result I wanted a small family environment; peace and quiet, and my own privacy.

My ex-wife and I did not know how to meet each other's needs because we were not aware of them.

I met one couple that was having marital issues. The young man felt that he was doing everything right in his marriage, yet, she began to distance herself from him. His wife was a single mother of four young children when they met. She was honest with him and told him that she did not want to have any more children. Though he was a few years' younger than her, he accepted her wishes that they not have kids of his own and married her any way. He truly loved her.

We spoke briefly about his childhood experience. His mother was a single parent and he witnessed his mother in relationships with abusive men. He had no formal concept or experience growing up of how a family was supposed to function. He struggled seeing his mother in and out of relationships never knowing that there was such a thing as marriage.

He was exposed to marriage later in life, but he struggled with the idea even though he agreed to honor her request of not having more children. Her children were older and they too had no interactions with their biological father.

The young man was so in love with the idea of marriage and having a family without knowing it that it created conflict with his wife. His expression of love towards his wife was to continually shower her with gifts. He was a hard-working individual who migrated to this country with only the shirt on his back. He is now the owner of a small construction company and financially stable.

He would work long hours to provide her with a nice home, and take care of her, and her children. On the days that he could rest, instead of romancing the wife, he used the time to have family activities such as weekend trips to a theme park or camping.

I first noticed the wife's frustration when she could not figure out the new smartphone that he had just purchased for her. In her frustration, she asked me if I knew how to work the phone. She stated that she was just getting used to the last model when the new model phone came out.

He wanted her to have the latest phone on the market and also bought her a brand-new smartwatch to go with the phone. She, unintentionally, opened her thoughts to me by letting me know how he is constantly buying her things about which she could care less. She stated that he spoils her kids the same way.

I asked her: "What was the problem with him spoiling her and her kids?" She paused and thought about her response. She did not know how to respond.

She then began to tell me, how this new movie was coming out this weekend and he had made plans to take her and the kids to dinner. After dinner, they were going to go to the movies. She said she was tired and didn't want to go out, and he became upset with her. She explained that he often gets upset when she tells him she does not want to go out.

I asked her how long they have been married. She said: "Four years now!" I asked her if she loved him. She began to explain that she loved him very much! He was a great man and a great husband. She had been in many abusive relationships and never met someone who treated her so well. She loved the fact that he was always attentive to her needs.

Again, I asked, what is the problem? She said she didn't know why she felt so frustrated?

I asked her when was the last time that she went out on a date as a couple. She laughed and said: "We have not been on a date since we married." She had a flashback moment and started telling me of all the things they would do together! She felt happy and alive! She said this was the first time someone had ever loved her as he did. So, when do you think the change started taking place, I asked? She paused for a moment.

"After dating for a year, we decided to move in together. Before we moved in, I began to introduce him to my kids. Once we moved in together, the focus shifted from me to my kids. Shortly after, we would no longer go out on dates." She enjoyed that he accepted her kids and that her kids grew attached to him – that is when she no longer felt like a wife, but a mother.

I knew what was going on! The man went into overdrive and shifted from husband, and lover, to a family man without him knowing it.

I asked if I could talk to the husband alone. She pleaded please do. I told her I believe I may know what the problem is; he is so in love with the "Idea of Marriage," that he has forgotten how to love you as an individual. He was so infatuated with the idea of having a family, that everything that they did, he wanted to do it as a family.

He slowly shifted his focus from that of his wife, whom he fell in love with, to the children. He shifted gears soon after marriage from being lover to stepfather and fell in love with the concept of family.

She began to tear up! That is exactly how I feel. I spent several weeks talking to the young man. I got him to open to me about his past. My conclusion was right: he was in love with the idea of marriage and had no concept of what a marriage truly was. He felt an overwhelming joy doing things as a family that he had forgotten about his wife's needs.

Then again, I have a good friend who was infatuated with a girl from high school. They were friends but he never got the courage to ask her to be his girlfriend. They remained friends throughout high school until, on his senior year, his family decided to move to another state losing contact for a number of years. Each eventually married and soon divorced. He divorced with no kids, and she divorced with kids.

Years later, they coincidently moved to the same state and same city. They met through mutual friends and were reunited. Their encounter sparked old feelings each had for one another. They both had feelings for each other, but because they were young, they did not know how to express them.

They went on a few dates and felt they were meant to be with each other. They quickly married without hesitation. After the first year of marriage, the couple began to encounter difficulties. The wife had constant conflicts with the father of her children. Her children wanted to live with their father, but she was refusing. My friend had his own internal conflicts. He enjoyed the company of other women. His wife suspected him of being unfaithful but my friend was very good at hiding his affairs.

They divorced shortly after their third year of marriage. They felt, because of the feelings they had for one another all throughout high school and because they knew each other, it was enough to get married. After all, they had feelings for each other.

People change with time. The person that you may have known five or ten years ago may not be the same person today. After my friend moved away his senior year, his heart was broken. He tried to heal his broken heart with other women, but he could never find someone whom he had the same feelings for as his high school crush. He eventually grew accustomed to enjoy women for just a short time until he grew tired and wanted to try someone new.

He was unfaithful to his first wife, and now with his second wife. His now ex-wife had a history of choosing the wrong men. Her first husband was very controlling and manipulative. Each spouse had a dark history that they failed to disclose. They never took the time to discover how much they had changed over the years before deciding to get married. They were both in love with the idea of marrying their high school crush and have a fairy tale wedding and life.

I have been familiar with men who are afraid of commitment. I have an uncle who is in every sense a "Ladies Man." He is so confident in himself, that he can approach women, and get them to fall in love with him. Time after time, these women become jealous and fearful of losing him. They truly believe that my uncle loves them. He makes them feel like he's the greatest thing that has ever happened to them. They do everything they can to prevent him from running off, and into the arms of other women.

In their attempt to hold on to him, they would take care of his every need. My uncle is a gigolo! They buy him clothes; they feed his addictions, and they cater to all his sexual needs. There a time-bomb waiting to explode.

It's only a matter of time, when these women realize that my uncle is lazy. They start to realize that this is not the man of their dreams, and he is nothing close to a father figure to their kids. After these women realize that they became infatuated with him, they kick him to the curb, and he is off seeking his next victim.

My uncle's life was no different than mine. After all, my life was modeled after his, my other three uncles, and my grandfather who was also a lady's man.

My uncle had no idea of what it meant to be a husband or a father. He had a hole in his heart that he could never satisfy. He thought being the world's greatest lover would bring him the love that he had always sought. He could never fill that void. He had countless women in his life, yet, he was always lonely and searching.

My older brother was fortunate enough not to have gotten his high school girlfriend pregnant. He was a high school football player that drove all the girls wild. He became sexually active at a very young age. It was impressive to see how his friends would host parties on a Friday or Saturday night, and specifically ask my brother to come.

They knew that if my brother would come, he would bring a group of girls with him. My brother was able to take advantage of the situation. He grew up under the same financial circumstances as I did. We had to fight for the clothes we wanted wear. Not having anything to wear to these parties, his friends would offer to buy him clothes. His friends would give him money for gas, and money to spend just so he would show up with girls to the party.

My brother became so used to people catering to his needs, because of the ability to attract girls, that it made it difficult for him to become independent. He never had a need to go out and work. What was the point if he was living for free?

He eventually met this young girl, a cousin of one of his best friends. She was a very beautiful girl! Her mom, his best friend's aunt, fell in love with me. She saw something different in me and tried to encourage her daughter to talk to me.

She would always ask me what I thought about her daughter but I was not confident enough to speak up. The daughter fell in love with my brother and they had begun a relationship for a number of years. During their high-school years, their relationship was fine. They would spend every day together. My brother never worked, so he would dedicate his life to her. He never had money and didn't need it; they were in love and just happy being with each other.

He had gotten so used to everyone catering to his needs that it became an illness. As the years passed, his girlfriend was maturing and beginning to notice my brother's behavior. She was a beautiful young lady that was starting to come into adulthood.

She started to notice that my brother was not the type of person she would want in her life as a husband or father to children. She started asking him to buy her things knowing that he did not have the means to give them to her. She was testing him to see if he would make some changes in his life. Knowing he could not give her the life that she desired; he attempted to sell illegal drugs, but was not successful.

Since he was well known, he was able to sell drugs and make money; the problem was that, whatever profit he made, he would spend it on his girlfriend. In his attempt to provide her with the life she desired, he started a life of crime. He would steal, rob, and break into houses.

He was so "In Love" with the idea of marriage that he would do what it took to give her what she asked for hoping she would fall deeper in love with him. He wanted to marry her. She was the love of his life. The problem stemmed in that she knew what she wanted. She had come from a good family. Her family had their dysfunctions, but she had a great family background.

She loved my brother and wanted him to be the man of her dreams, and possibly marry him! My brother was never exposed to a healthy marriage or a family. He was only able to love her, based on his idea of love and marriage.

In her disappointment, she met someone whom she felt would be an ideal husband. She became pregnant by him, a Black American man, and did not know how to end things with my brother. My brother was so in love with her that he could not accept that he was not the father of the child. He was informed by several family members that she had been seen with the other man but he would not accept what everyone could see until the birth of the child.

She had an attachment to my mother even though she had her difficulties with my brother. She asked my mother to be present at the time of the delivery. When the baby was delivered, my mother informed my brother: "He was not the father of the baby!" He became upset with her and insisted on being the father. He held the baby firmly and assured everyone that it was his.

Shortly after, a black male came to the hospital with flowers and balloons. He was there to see his baby, who had just been born.

There was a heated exchange of words between my brother and the man and security was called. They were both escorted out of the hospital, before it turned into a physical altercation.

His girlfriend confessed at that moment that she no longer loved him and he was not the father of the baby. It took my brother weeks for him to accept that the person whom he loved chose to marry another man.

My brother was a victim of being in love with the idea of marriage! He loved his girlfriend and always talked about marrying her. He only had an idea of marriage and did not know how to make his idea a reality.

At a young age, he had made it clear to my mother that it was not his responsibility to care for her kids. He decided to live his life the way he wanted to live. His life was built on being dependent on his friends giving him money for clothes and food. His roots were not properly planted.

If you were to ask my brother to this day, he would be too proud, or too hurt to admit it, but he still loves her. I believe he is still in love with her, because she was his attempt to have a family of his own.

Sitcoms were a wonderful attempt to introduce people to what an ideal American family is. They were indeed great shows. The sad truth is… there is a large population of Americans that can only dream of having a family just like the ones on television. It introduced me to an idea that I desired so much that I was willing to rush into it without much consideration, in spite of the fact that it was difficult to obtain. I based my ideal marriage and family off a television show.

Sarah was met with disappointment. She had doubted that she was able to have a child at her age. She decided to ask her husband to take one of her maids in an attempt to give him a son. This created some conflict. She thought that she could handle the idea of having a son from a different woman. After her son Isaac was born, the Bible tells us that Sarah told Abraham that he needed to send away the Egyptian woman and her son Ismael. "And Sarah saw the son of Hagar the Egyptian, whom she had borne to Abraham, scoffing (Gen. 21:9 NKJV)."

Sarah was a woman who had some dysfunctions in her life. It is hard to know if she held resentment and anger towards Abraham for not protecting her against the Pharaoh. Besides all the wealth Abraham had been blessed with, she was not happy. After she conceived, God changed her name and gave her a new life, yet, she could not get over her past mistakes. She felt threatened by the boy because he was a reminder of her mistakes.

We all have some form of dysfunctions in our lives whether we inherited it, or because of a mistake that we made. As humans, we can feel threatened by our past mistakes – the shame and guilt can be overpowering if we do not deal with it.

We should never be ashamed of our past or try to hide it. The purpose of marriage is to help one another. If you are weak in an area, the spouse should be able to identify and help balance the marriage. The only way that there can be balance is by being open and honest about past mistakes and failures in spite of the fear of losing the spouse.

Everyone has their own idea of what marriage is. How to turn the idea of marriage into a concept is a lifelong learning event that takes work and dedication.

We cannot do it on our own. You married to have someone help carry the load.

Chapter 14

There Is Still Hope

God has led me through a wonderful journey. Through all the pain and all the losses, I truly am grateful for the wonderful life I have. As I walk closer to God, I am finally able to realize that, He has allowed me to pass through a process that helped me to discover not only what was buried deep inside, but what had plagued my family for generations.

The Bible states: "And we know that all things work together for good to those who love God, to those who are the called according to His purpose (Rom. 8:28 NKJV).

As I was going through my journey, I would stand in awe seeing how God was revealing things to me, I felt unworthy. Yet, on many other occasions I would question God every step of the way. Why did God allow me to experience so much pain and loss? What good will come from all of this?

Jesus one day was discussing the parable of the seed to his disciples. He made it clear:

"Most assuredly, I say to you, unless a grain of wheat falls into the ground and dies, it remains alone; but if it dies, it produces much grain, (JN. 12:24 NKJV).

There were many nights in which I had asked God to take me to heaven with him. I felt like I was dying. The pain; the depression, and the inability to see the light of hope seemed so far off. Some nights, I would cry myself to sleep hoping not to wake up in the morning. I felt so weak and lost. But it was all necessary. I did not understand the process! At one point, I asked God, if you have a plan for me, I do not want any part of it, please choose someone else, and stop the pain. It was necessary that a part of me die.

Nine years after my divorce, God was finally beginning to deal with me. For the first four years after my divorce, I was so angry with God. I felt that He had abandoned me. I would attend church, but I was struggling spiritually. I never stopped loving God; I just felt I was of no use to Him anymore. What good could come out of all of this? Could I still bear fruit?

As you read my journey, you can come to understand that my journey has a purpose. I have so many unanswered questions that I may never get a response to, but had I not passed through this process, I would have probably ended up in a worse situation.

We are living in a difficult time. It is common to see more and more people choosing to live together instead of committing to marriage. Surprisingly, these couples stay committed to each other all their lives. The devil has been working hard to destroy the basis of what God created, man and woman to unite as one flesh in holy matrimony. People do not want to marry anymore! People believe that marriage is unnecessary.

Today, there are phone apps that have been designed for two people to come together for "One-night stands." They could care less about committing to a relationship. Someone mentioned that we are living in a "Throw-away" society in which, no one wants to fight for what they believe anymore. What's the point of fighting anymore?

Instead of fighting, they throw away what they feel no longer works in their lives. It is so common to see single fathers now because the mothers want to enjoy the single life. Family values and good morals are no longer instilled in children.

To make a positive change in our society, we need to bring positive balance into this world. There is still hope for a great future. If you are reading this and you are faith-based, you will know that Jesus Christ is still alive and working in us.

He is still offering an eternal love that is pure, and the hope that we can have a great marriage and a great family. Not all is lost! As believers, if we build our lives based on His pure love, we in turn, can pour out that love into the person whom God has placed in our path to love and eventually marry.

I have often heard people say to me in conversations as to the reason they do not wish to bring children into this world. These are great young couples with good solid foundations of love. Their reason is because the world continues to worsen with each passing of days that they do not want to bring children into a world like this. It is true, this world, and our society have been deteriorating at a rapid pace over the past years.

My response to them is simple: - "If we want this world to become a great place, we have to encourage that behavior. You're a young model couple with great morals and values that can bring a good person into this dying world to bring balance and hope."

If you are not faith-based and are reading this, there is still hope and the ability to find pure love within your marriage. There is no need to rush into love and marriage. Love can grow if you properly feed it, guide it, protect it, and trim the areas that can cause damage to its roots.

During the 18th century, courtship was the process of getting to know someone with the intent of building a strong foundation of love. Courtship was often supervised by parents, or someone close to the family to ensure at the courting process was pure.

Parents would allow the couple a number of years to get to know each other. When the couple would finally commit to being espoused, they would come together knowing they were committing to a life-long commitment.

The Natives of America going from the North down to South America often had the right of passage rituals that the young men and women had to endure, before attempting to consider marriage. The young men had to prove themselves by enduring nights in the jungle on their own. They had to prove they were capable of living independently and able to provide for their spouse to be.

There is a tribe in the Amazons of South America where the young ladies are gathered around the elders of the tribes. They sit the young girls in the middle as the elder's huddle around. They then begin to pluck out the hairs off of their heads, until they are completely bald. If the young ladies can endure the hardship, they are deemed ready for marriage.

Today, it is easy to find someone who attracts you, whether it is a physical attraction or emotional attraction. With social media and the internet so available, finding a mate is not a problem. People do not have to work anymore for relationship. All they have to do is click "Like!"

This generation does not value the covenant of marriage anymore. They feel if a marriage isn't working, divorce and move on to the next, or better yet, why marry. Young women should not make it easy for young men to date them, let alone marry them. Guys should not jump at the first girl who smiles at them and ask them to marry them.

If you are a parent, it's your job to teach your children how much they are worth and how they should be valued! If you teach your children that they are highly valued, the person whom they choose to date will have to value them just as they high. As parents, we need to set high standards for our children!

The Bible is a fascinating book. It's a book of life that brings wisdom and guidance to our souls. We read stories of men like Isaac (in the book of Genesis) who had to wait for years before "his" father (Abraham) decided he was ready for marriage. His father set rules for his son and how to go about choosing his wife.

His first rule was that the women chosen for his son had to come from "his" father's house, *but you shall go to my country and to my family, and take a wife for my son Isaac,* (Gen. 24:4 NKJV)." The servant who was sent to seek out a wife for his son, journeyed far to seek her out. I can only imagine the anticipation Isaac must have had awaiting his bride to come. He was not only subjected to wait, but his wife also had to be chosen for him. He did not have the luxury of just choosing the first woman that presented herself, or was appealing to the eyes.

Isaac was the first case in which we see, "Good things come to those that wait."

His father's servant also put conditions for the woman who was to be chosen. The woman had to have been a servant first before a wife. He asked God, "The women who offered to water the camels, let her be the one (Gen. 24:44 NKJV)."

Jacob, the grandson of Abraham had to endure fourteen years of labor before he finally was able to marry the woman whom he loved so much (Gen. 28:18-30 NKJV). Moses, during his years living with all the wealth of Egypt, was not able to find a wife. It was not until he became a shepherd in the desert that his father-n-law

Jethro allowed him to marry his daughter, *"Then Moses was content to live with the man, and he gave Zipporah his daughter to Moses (Ex.2:21 NKJV)."*

Why do we want to rush into marriage?

I read somewhere once, "There is no such thing of perfect marriage, the only thing that exists, are couples who refuse to give up."

Every year at the church, we hold marriage conferences. It's a cliché for the speaker to ask the audience if there are couples who have been married for more than twenty-five years to stand up. They then proceed to ask several couples what they think is the "Secret" to having a long lasting relationship. Every couple will give you their own opinion of what has worked for them. The one thing that they will all agree is that it has not been easy.

Every couple has had their battles, and many have the scars to prove it.

Marriage is not a means of escape. You cannot run to marriage hoping to have a better life. You do not create a marriage, you build one. My pastor once said, "There's no secret to a healthy marriage, you just have to want it, and work hard for it."

If you married because you were "In Love with Marriage," you still have an opportunity to turn your idea into a concept. My recommendations for you if you are faith-based is going to be, "Fall in love with the author and creator of love, God Himself!" You cannot offer to someone what you do not have. If you want to love, love God first.

In doing so, you will fill your life with His love. You will start expressing that love to yourselves first, and then towards others. Eventually, that love will be committed and expressed solely to that one special person, who will also share that same love with you.

If you are not faith-based, I am going to recommend spending time with yourself, discover yourself, and find ways of breaking bad habits that you feel will be a hindrance in your relationship. Dig into your family roots, and find out if there has been anything within your family, that has not allowed your family to have a healthy and prosperous life. Break any generational curses that may want to present themselves when you decide to engage in courting or marriage.

Work towards building yourself up and your goals. Read books about marriage and discover what your idea of marriage is and create a plan. Once you have an idea, learn how you can turn it into a concept. We all have something great to offer and share with a special person. We must ensure that we should engage in cleaning ourselves first, so that we do not bring our mess into the lives of your spouse and the lives of your children.

Spend time talking to a pastor or licensed mental health coach before marriage, just to make sure you are ready for marriage. It's a small investment that will serve a good purpose for your future. Once you feel that you can start the process of selecting a person you want to date, set boundaries and high standards for yourself.

Be sure to know what is it that you are looking for in a mate, and when you find someone who can identify with what you are presenting, ask them what their standards and boundaries may be, so that together you can work to see what your compatibility is with each other.

If the person you are considering has not set standards or boundaries for themselves, they may not hold themselves at a high value as you do yourself. You will almost certainly fail if you decide to base your courtship on the physical or intellectual attractiveness.

Always remember… our bodies are subjected to deterioration. What look's nice today may not always be the case years later. What will remain is going to be that profound love you feel for one another.

Once you have decided on a suitable mate, take the time to date. Ask questions! Find out what they expect from one another if they decide to marry. Dig into their family history to see if there is a pattern of hindrances. If the person chooses not to disclose any family history, I would remind the person that you are trying to build a relationship, built on trust and communication. They may be too ashamed to talk about their family.

Everyone has a past, and not everyone's family is perfect. We are not looking for the perfect person to marry. The goals and the idea is to discover each other's weak areas and provide support or assurance that together, you can overcome the past, correct the future, and ensure that the past has stayed buried and does not try to make its way into your marriage.

Talk to each other about what your ideas of marriage. Try to get each other's view of how they have modeled or, would like to model their marriage? This will eliminate misunderstandings of what the other person thought they were getting into.

Once the decision has been made to marry, evaluate and determine if your love is deep and pure so that you will be able to work, and support each other anticipating the difficulties when they will present themselves.

Spend time with couples that have been married for more than twenty years. Do not be afraid to ask them questions and ask for their advice. This will not guarantee that your marriage will be long-lasting as theirs, but it will allow you to take all the necessary precautions to ensure that you have done everything according to you faith, or your morals and values.

Once you are married... enjoy the marriage!

Do not rush into children, so that you can enjoy the time together. Once children come, there is another set of challenges. Work will now become a priority during that time. You will now have to encounter the challenges of being tired, dealing with the children, and dealing with the needs of the home. This is where couples often put their marriage on the back seat, and attend more to the family then the marriage.

Once you have started your marriage, make it a goal to never stop dating!

If the wife is overly protective of the baby and is not willing to leave the baby with a sitter or family member, while you go out on a date night, find ways to make a date night at home.

A good friend of mine has been married for over twenty years. The couple has their date nights at home. They have five children together, so the finances are tight. Their date night consists of the oldest child taking care of the younger siblings. They enter their room, and lock the door. They order out food and watch a movie. They enjoy their time together without the hindrance of their children even though they are close by. The children know they are not allowed to knock or call them on their cell phones.

If you want to remain in love with your spouse, make sure they are a continuous priority in your life. The children will be an important part of your family, but always remember: your children will grow older, and eventually marry and move away.

Your life will be spent with your spouse. They will be the one person whom you should always count on to never leave your side! Your spouse will have to deal with your character for years to come. They are the last person you should be offending!

Dating your spouse after marriage is so critical.

Psychologists state that people change every three to five years. Their likes and desires; their behaviors, their maturity, and even intimacy changes. Dating your spouse allows you know to understand their changes, and helps you to work with the changes.

Dating your spouse ensures that the communication within the marriage is constantly open. Be open and honest with your spouse about the changes you are experiencing, and encourage your spouse to open up to their changes as well.

Do not fear introducing new techniques into your sexual life, as both men and women grow weary from monotony; there are no rules in keeping it exciting. Never allow you or your spouse to feel intimidated by the changes that life brings, whether emotionally or physically. Earn a Ph.D. degree in falling in love with your spouse!

Allow your marriage to be a successful one founded on true love! Being in love with marriage is a wonderful thing, so long as you do not forget to include your spouse in that love.

If you are reading this because you may have, or are going through some difficulties in your marriage, I want to reassure you that not all hope is lost. If you are reading this and your marriage has already ended, there is still hope!

A break-up, a separation, and even a divorce do not indicate that it's the end of your life. You can still get up and recover. There is still time for you to reevaluate your situation, and figure out what it is that you want most in life? Sometimes, it takes a situation like this to allow you to understand, and discover what has been buried deep inside of you that needs to come out?

These situations are never easy, but vital, and necessary so that we can dig in, and dig up, our past, and make the necessary changes to fix our current situation and our future.

To conclude, I would like to introduce a brief introduction to the next series of discussions I will be presenting. This topic deals with the faith-based side of what a spiritual leader and watchman consist of. Marriage and a family is a wonderful blessing that can be given to couples. Like all treasures in life, there will always be a temptation for someone to desire what you have, and would stop at nothing to steal your love and marriage from you.

The Bible teaches us, "The thief does not come except to steal, and to kill, and to destroy. I have come that they may have life, and that they may have it more abundantly, (JN. 10:10, NKJV)." As a priest and spiritual leader of the home, you must be continually watching, and praying over your family to ward off any attacks that may come from the devil, and any thieves wanting to rob you of your blessings.

Not only are you called to love your spouse as biblically commanded, but you also need to protect your spouse, your family, and your home. This is part of the priesthood of the home!

I pray that these words have been an inspiration to you during your time of need, or you may feel they can greatly benefit someone who is going through some difficulties in their marriage.

Never be discouraged from seeking professional help!

I love my pastor and my church, but my pastor can agree that there are certain areas in which he is not able to provide further help and will encourage you to seek the opinion of an expert, and licensed professional in the area that you may need.

God bless you and may the Lord's favor and blessing be upon you and your family! May the Lord bless you and prosper you in all that you do, whether in deed or word. To God be the glory!

2 Chronicles 7:14 (NKJV)

If My people who are called by My name will humble themselves, and pray and seek My face, and turn from their wicked ways, then I will hear from heaven, and will forgive their sin and heal their land..

Author's Bio

My name is Jessie Garcia. I have served as an Ordained Minister in the oldest Spanish-speaking Oneness Pentecostal denomination in the United States, the Apostolic Assembly of the Faith in Christ Jesus (Apostolic Assembly).

My theological studies were obtained through International Apostolic Bible College (CBAI). I have served in the ministry for twenty-two years of which four years were spent as an Associate Pastor. I continue to serve passionately as a minister at the local level.

My first years in the ministry, God had chosen me to serve the church, the ministry, and the community. God has shifted the focus to the area of marriage where many couples are in need for counseling.

God has led many individuals into my life in this ministry of service. Through my experiences, God has prepared me to see their needs and enabled me to be a blessing in their marriage, before I knew that God had a purpose for my pain.

As I asked God one day as to the purpose of my pain, He directed me to:

2Cor. 1:3-4"Blessed be God, even the Father of our Lord Jesus Christ, the Father of mercies, and the God of all comfort; Who comforteth us in all our tribulation, that we may be able to comfort them which are in any trouble, by the comfort wherewith we ourselves are comforted of God. (KVJ)"

God put me in a position in which I could only focus on writing this book, "In Love with Marriage," which opened my life to a new ministry. God used this book to show me that even through all my mistakes, He still has a purpose for me and can still use me in ways I could not imagine.

Pure Thoughts Publishing LLC